EXPERIENCE

PARIS

⊙ Walking Eye App

Your Insight Guide now includes a free app and eBook, dedicated to your chosen destination, all included for the same great price as before. They are available to download from the free Walking Eye container app in the App Store and Google Play. Simply download the Walking Eye container app to access the eBook and app dedicated to your purchased book. The app features an up-to-date A to Z of travel tips, information on events, activities and destination highlights, as well as hotel, restaurant and bar listings. See below for more information and how to download.

MULTIPLE DESTINATIONS AVAILABLE

Now that you've bought this book you can download the accompanying destination app and eBook for free. Inside the Walking Eye container app, you'll also find a whole range of other Insight Guides destination apps and eBooks, all available for purchase.

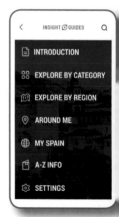

DEDICATED SEARCH OPTIONS

Use the different sections to browse the places of interest by category or region, or simply use the 'Around me' function to find places of interest nearby. You can then save your selected restaurants, bars and activities to your Favourites or share them with friends using email, Twitter and Facebook.

FREQUENTLY UPDATED LISTINGS

Restaurants, bars and hotels change all the time. To ensure you get the most out of your guide, the app features all of our favourites, as well as the latest openings, and is updated regularly. Simply update your app when you receive a notification to access the most current listings available.

TRAVEL TIPS & DESTINATION OVERVIEWS

The app also includes a complete A to Z of handy travel tips on everything from visa regulations to local etiquette. Plus, you'll find destination overviews on shopping, sport, the arts, local events, health, activities and more.

HOW TO DOWNLOAD THE WALKING EYE

Available on purchase of this guide only.
1. Visit our website: www.insightguides.com/walkingeye
2. Download the Walking Eye container app to your smartphone (this will give you access to both the destination app and the eBook)
3. Select the scanning module in the Walking Eye container app
4. Scan the QR code on this page – you will be asked to enter a verification word from the book as proof of purchase
5. Download your free destination app* and eBook for travel information on the go

* Other destination apps and eBooks are available for purchase separately or are free with the purchase of the Insight Guide book

Travel
914.43604
Edw
2016

CONTENTS

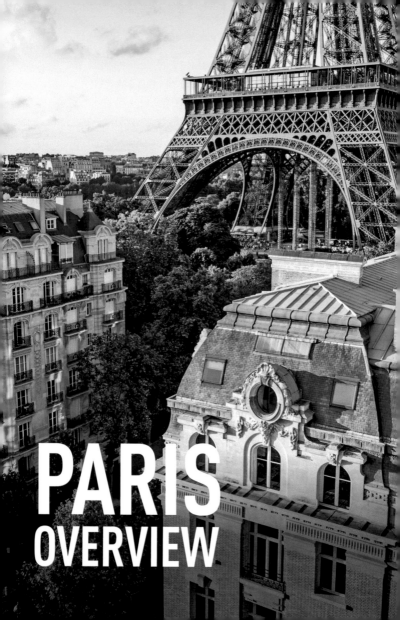

PARIS
OVERVIEW

Capital of romance, of fashion, of food, of intellectuals and philosophers, famed for its historic buildings and monuments and for that indefinable *je ne sais quoi* that makes up French chic, Paris is a city that likes to live up to its myths; but it is also a modern working city, of financial institutions, of scientific discoveries and learned research institutes.

Don't be fooled into thinking of Paris as a museum. Paris has always modernised, over the centuries expanding in concentric circles outwards from the Ile de la Cité, and has never been afraid to drop in radical new monuments or reinvent old ones. On the one hand you can find Roman baths sticking up in the middle of a Gothic mansion, on the other the glass pyramid at the Louvre and a futuristic ship designed by Frank Gehry that has just 'sailed' into the Bois de Boulogne. Two of the most recent cultural venues occupy both a converted theatre and a covered market, new parks have been created around the city's edges, and an entire new district is taking root above old railway sidings around the new Bibliothèque Nationale, along the Seine.

If there is one recommended requisite to making the most of the city, it is curiosity. This is a place where you come to admire the grand facades and imperious vistas, the world-renowned museums and glorious churches – but must also be everready to peer through carriage doorways or wander down passageways to discover the hidden gardens, concealed houses and workshops that make up the private, intimate Paris behind the bravura. One of the most appealing aspects of the city is that it is intensely lived in. Part of the fun of wandering round the streets is discovering the local street market, the favourite spot for a coffee and the best baker. Undeterred by the 2015 terrorist attacks, residents continue to privilege what they call the *'style de vie'* – lifestyle – which means that for all the apparent rush, there is always time to stroll around the food market or sit at a café terrace for coffee or an apéritif.

IN THE MOOD FOR...

... GASTRONOMY

Evidence of the Parisians' love of food can be seen everywhere from street markets and busy lunchtime cafés to grand dining establishments. While the image relayed abroad is often of elitist grand dining involving squadrons of waiters and silver cloches – awarded Unesco heritage status in 2010 – and once-in-a-lifetime meals in the sumptuous surroundings of **Le Grand Véfour** (see page 51) or **Pierre Gagnaire** (see page 71), the reality is much more varied and depends on your mood or budget. The mainstay are bistros and brasseries, trad places such as **Bistrot Paul Bert** (see page 105), **La Fontaine de Mars** (see page 141), or budget institution **Chartier** (see page 62). However many bistros are renewing the genre, mixing tradition with modern seasonal dishes at **Astier** (see page 105), **Mon Vieil Ami** (see page 32), 'bistronomiques' like **Chez L'Ami Jean** (see page 141) or Christian Constant's chic diner **Les Cocottes** (see page 141) – always with an emphasis on quality ingredients but retaining the informal mood and reasonable prices.

... ROMANCE

Paris enjoys an image as one of the world's most romantic cities, yet what makes it romantic is hard to pin down. Rather, it all comes down to an endless collection of the smallest things: misty early morning views of the quais of **Ile St-Louis** (see page 32), the glamour of watching opera or ballet ensconced in red satin and velvet in a box at **Palais Garnier** (see page 57), relaxing in the beautiful, intimate square that is **place des Vosges** (see page 34) with its red brick arcades, the timeless charm of a stroll along the **Canal St-Martin** (see page 102) or the pathos of the **cemetery at Montmartre** (see page 87). Then again, romance might come in the shape of a grand summer meal for two under a parasol in the gardens at **Laurent** (see page 71), or as a memorable stay in a fine hotel – in the dimly lit, blood red Classic Suite at **Hôtel Costes** (see page 54), where the downstairs rose shop has dozens of beautiful blooms for an impressive, impromptu bouquet, or the indulgence of beams and luscious fabrics at the **Hôtel du Petit Moulin** (see page 42).

... RETAIL THERAPY

Paris lives up to its reputation as a fashion capital with the couture houses of **avenue Montaigne** (see page 70) and cutting-edge cuts at **Palais-Royal** (see page 58). Those who want to keep track of trends follow groundbreaking concept store **Colette** (see page 54) and its alter ego **Merci** (see page 42). And while the *grands magasins* (see page 63) offer an awe-inspiring choice, the charm of Paris shopping lies in the city's boutiques: say **Abou d'Abi Bazar** or **Matières à Réflexion** in the Haut-Marais (see page 42), or kitchen emporium **E Dehillerin** (see page 56), an endearing relic of the Les Halles market.

... OBSERVING PARISIANS

What could be more Parisian than watching Parisians? Parisians excel at it, sitting on café terraces to see and be seen. Maybe that's what café society is all about: spotting famous faces at **Café de Flore** and **Les Deux Magots** (see page 122), sizing up the fashion brigade at **L'Avenue** (see page 70), inspecting other people's purchases at **Café Charlot** (see page 42). Catch the diversity of streetlife at **Marché d'Aligre** (see page 101) or **Abbesses** (see page 85), children and charmers in the **Jardin du Luxembourg** (see page 124), smart families in **Parc Monceau** (see page 76), and trendies at **Chez Jeannette** (see page 94).

... A VIEW

Remember that Paris once boasted the tallest building in the world – the **Eiffel Tower** (see page 136) – and you'll realise that there are plenty of things to climb here: the steep tower of **Notre-Dame Cathedral** (see page 28), the gazebo in **Parc des Buttes-Chaumont** (see page 104), the dome of the **Panthéon** (see page 118). Some of the best views are the panoramas afforded by the city's hills – from the top of the steps leading up to the **Sacré-Cœur** (see page 90), zooming into the

city centre from the **Parc de Belleville** (see page 106), across the Seine from the **Domaine de St-Cloud** (see page 162). Perfect vantage points are often to be found not too high up but at roof level: ideal for glimpses of private lives in apartments and secret roof gardens; try the summer rooftop restaurants at **Galeries Lafayette** and **Printemps** (see page 63), or the escalator ride up the **Centre Pompidou** (see page 36), where the city spreads out before you as you rise and you can dine with a view at Georges restaurant.

... FAMILY FUN

Paris is a family-friendly city awash with parks and climbing frames and those with kids have a great excuse to go up the **Eiffel Tower** (see page 136). The **Jardin des Plantes** (see page 114) is good for all ages with the Ménagerie and brilliantly displayed Grande Galerie de l'Evolution. There are special children's sections at the **Cité des Sciences** (see page 154) and fun playgrounds outside. Bigger kids get a thrill from the prison cells at the **Conciergerie** (see page 30), macabre bones at **Les Catacombes** (see page 143) or vintage flying machines at the **Musée des Arts et Métiers** (see page 45). Don't be intimidated by the size of the large museums: the **Centre Pompidou** (see page 36) has specially conceived exhibitions in its Galerie des Enfants, there are Impressionists galore at **Musée d'Orsay** (see page 132), and all the Egyptian mummies a child could desire at the **Louvre** (see page 50). This is also a good city for eating out with kids – do as the Parisians do. Go for bustle and spectacle at **La Coupole** brasserie (see page 142), friendly **Astier** (see page 105) or budget legend **Chartier** (see page 62), for watching the waiter memorise the orders.

... FINE ART

The **Louvre** (see page 50) is the super museum to beat all museums, the **Centre Pompidou** (see page 36) feels like a voyage through modern art, and there are also major temporary exhibitions on show at the **Grand Palais** (see page 68) and the **Musée d'Art Moderne de la Ville de Paris** (see page 74). For contemporary art, see what's happening at the new **Fondation Louis Vuitton** (see page 150), the **Palais de Tokyo** (see page 74), or hit the preview circuit at the **Marais private galleries** (see page 41) and the new galleries colonising **Belleville** (see page 106). Impressionism was perhaps the Parisian art movement par excellence, and superb collections are to be found at **Musée d'Orsay** (see page 132), **Musée Marmottan Monet** (see page 150) and the **Orangerie** (see page 55). Individual collectors have made their mark at **Musée Jaquemart-André** (see page 72), with gems of the Italian Renaissance, or **Musée Maillol** (see page 138), while houses and studios impart a personal insight into the life of the artist at the eccentric **Musée Gustave Moreau** (see page 86), the atmosphere of an old Montparnasse artist's studio at **Musée Bourdelle** (see page 145) or the sheer virtuosity and creativity of Auguste Rodin at **Musée Rodin** (see page 135).

... MULTICULTURAL PARIS

Paris has always drawn in migrants but probably never more so than today, a history traced at the **Cité de l'Immigration** (see page 157). The tower blocks of **Chinatown** (see page 158) harbour Chinese restaurants and exotic supermarkets, and Middle Europe meets North Africa in the Jewish food shops on **rue des Rosiers** (see page 38). Wander along **Faubourg-St-Denis** (see page 94), where a bar scene is developing amid ethnic grocers and Indian restaurants, and discover multicultural comic talent at **Le Comedy Club** (see page 60).

... OUTDOOR LAZING

In intensely lived in, densely populated Paris, where most Parisians are starved of gardens, the city does its best to make up for it with a panoply of squares, parks and playgrounds. Even in the city centre the pace slows down in tranquil, hidden spots like the **Arènes de Lutèce** (see page 119), while the **Jardin du Luxembourg** (see page 124) is just made for surveying the scene – lazily – from a Luxembourg chair. Paris is great for walking. Amble along the **Canal St-Martin** (see page 102) on a Sunday, to pause at canalside cafés or watch as barges chug through the locks.

... HISTORIC JOURNEYS

It can feel as if you are totally surrounded by history in Paris, simply by the airy beauty of **Notre-Dame** (see page 28), the golden facades of the **Marais mansions** (see page 33) or the unbelievable number of writers, politicians, generals, artists, singers and inventors who shaped the city resting in **Père Lachaise cemetery** (see page 108) or of great men honoured at the **Panthéon** (see page 118). There are traces of medieval and Roman Paris at the **Musée National du Moyen-Age** (see page 116), royal tombs at **St-Denis** (see page 161), royal residences at the **Château de Vincennes** (see page 163) and the **Louvre** (see page 50), and Napoleon at **Les Invalides** (see page 134). The Revolution of 1789 meanwhile is powerfully evoked in the prison cells of the **Conciergerie** (see page 30), and by the solitude of the **Chapelle Expiatoire** (see page 77) and **Cimetière de Picpus** (see page 100). Some things seem to have barely changed in centuries: the timewarped 17th-century perfection of **Ile St-Louis** (see page 32), the house of a mythic **Merveilleuse at the Petit Hôtel Bourrienne** (see page 95) – where Fortunée Hamelin entertained visitors from her bath, its gorgeous decor intact – or the incredible craftsmanship on view at the **Manufacture des Gobelins** (see page 120), a working historic factory.

IN THE MOOD FOR...

... A NIGHT OUT

Many bars and brasseries around town stay open until 1 or 2am. Young hipsters flock to the Canal St-Martin or Faubourg-St-Denis, while St-Germain has a more classic cocktail scene. Good rock venues include the **Trianon** and **La Cigale** in Pigalle (see page 91), while live music and clubbing thrives at **Batofar** (see page 127) as well as in other floating venues on the Seine, free from the noise restrictions of many districts. One of Paris's most surprising night spots is also on – or in – the river: **Showcase** (see page 69), hidden inside the Pont Alexandre III bridge.

... LITERARY INSPIRATION

Paris kicks off the September start of term with an outpouring of new books, and you'll still find writers today in the traditional publishing heartland of St-Germain, following Sartre and de Beauvoir to **Café de Flore** (see page 122). Hemingway and Orwell found literary inspiration – and cheap meals – around **place de la Contrescarpe** (see page 121) and you can sit at the same table as the former at **La Closerie des Lilas** (see page 142). Discover souvenirs of Victor Hugo at his **apartment** on elegant place des Vosges (see page 34), and George Sand's affair with Chopin at the **Musée de la Vie Romantique** (see page 88).

... MODERN ARCHITECTURE

Most people associate Paris with historic heritage, yet the city has never been afraid to inject the urban fabric with radical new buildings that initially shocked but have now been adopted, such as Rogers and Piano's exciting coloured tubes at the **Centre Pompidou** (see page 36) and I M Pei's glass pyramid at the **Louvre** (see page 50), joined more recently by the baroque form of Jean Nouvel's **Musée du Quai Branly** (see page 139). The latter's latest stamp on the city is the **Philharmonie de Paris** (see page 155) concert hall in **Parc de la**

Villette, which opened in 2015. Fans of the Modern Movement should head to the **Fondation Le Corbusier** (see page 151) and the **Cité Universitaire** (see page 151). Catch an overview of modern architecture at the **Cité de l'Architecture** (see page 73) and see a whole district in the making, growing up around the **Bibliothèque Nationale François Mitterrand** (see page 126).

... VILLAGE LIFE

Paris is often described as a collection of villages, each with its distinctive character and style, and many Parisians are intensely attached to their *quartier*. Some of these neighbourhoods were once bona fide villages, for instance **Charonne** (see page 156), **Batignolles** (see page 93) and hilly **Montmartre** (see page 84). Elsewhere it's a question of mood, a picturesque enclave such as **Quartier Mouzaïa** (see page 104), the alleyways of **Faubourg-St-Antoine** (see page 107) colonised by artists and designers, or the charm of the **Mouffetard district** (see page 121), with its much-loved markets.

... SCIENCE AND TECHNOLOGY

Paris's scientific heritage is often overlooked, yet the marks of engineering prowess are stamped all over the ironwork of the **Eiffel Tower** (see page 136) and the nave of the **Grand Palais** (see page 68), as well as unseen and underground in **Les Egouts** (see page 144), keeping the city functioning today. There are excellent science and technology collections at the **Cité des Sciences** (see page 154) and the **Musée des Arts et Métiers** (see page 45), botanists and zoologists based at the **Jardin des Plantes** (see page 114), while digital technology has the edge at the **Gaîté Lyrique** (see page 44).

... PARISIAN CHIC

If there's one word that is instantly associated with Parisiennes, it is 'chic'. An inimitable *je ne sais quoi* is achieved with the perfect accoutrements – perhaps a sublime handbag from **Balenciaga** (see page 70) or exclusive scent from **Serge Lutens** (see page 53), the indulgence of an orange flower-scented body scrub in the Spa at the **Four Seasons George V** (see page 79), elegantly packaged gâteaux from the **Pâtisserie des Rêves** (see page 140), lunch at **Mini Palais** (see page 68), or joining ladies who tea at the **Musée Jacquemart-André** (see page 72).

NEIGHBOURHOODS

With the River Seine running through the middle, Paris divides neatly into Right Bank (Rive Droite) to the north, traditionally associated with business and commerce, and intellectual, literary Left Bank (Rive Gauche) to the south; a collection of villages each with its own style, though a more truthful divide would perhaps be between wealthy west and poorer, working-class east.

The Islands and the Marais. In the heart of the city yet a world apart: Ile de la Cité is the centre of religious and legal Paris, while Ile St-Louis is a genteel 17th-century enclave. Across the water on the Right Bank, the Marais district was built up in the 16th and 17th centuries and happily escaped most of Baron Haussmann's urban projects – leaving intact stunning mansions of golden stone now colonised by gay bars, fashion boutiques and art galleries.

Louvre, Opéra and Grands Boulevards. The Louvre and Palais Garnier opera house epitomise the Paris of great royal and imperial monuments. But you'll also find entertainment along the Grands Boulevards, unusual covered passages traversing the financial district behind Palais Royal, and historic rue St-Honoré, a great shopping street.

Champs-Elysées and Monceau. The Champs-Elysées is flashy Paris, all luxury shops, lavish apartments and grand hotels. The area was transformed by the world fairs, and the flamboyant Grand Palais and the museums of Chaillot hill which came in their wake. Monceau is a monied, less showy area, concealing a romantic park and chic museums.

Montmartre and Pigalle. Montmartre does its best to convince you it's a rural hill village. More urban Pigalle, long associated with sleaze, is still a nightlife focus. To the south, little explored Nouvelle Athènes, two centuries ago an intellectual hub, and the gritty Gare du Nord hinterland are experiencing a bar and bobo (bourgeois-bohème) revival.

Bastille, Belleville and Ménilmontant. Bastille is the historic furniture-making district, peppered with craft workshops and symbol of the Revolution. Multicultural Ménilmontant and Belleville seem far from the Paris of Haussmann, with wildly contrasting public housing and villagey pockets. Here you'll find Père Lachaise cemetery, a new gallery district and cultural venues with an underground edge.

Latin Quarter, St-Germain and Seine. The Latin Quarter is historically the university quarter, where you'll find Roman remains, medieval streets, studenty bars and art cinemas mixed in with prestigious academic institutions and some of the city's loveliest churches. St-Germain is quintessential, international Left Bank, synonymous with café society, although a chic fashion set has rather replaced its literary clients.

Invalides and Montparnasse. To the east of Les Invalides, the mansions of Faubourg-St-Germain are home to ministries and discreet vieille France aristocracy; to the west is bourgeois residential territory, which often means good places to eat, plus a few oddities like the Eiffel Tower. Montparnasse spelled cosmopolitan, artistic Paris in the 1920s, and while the Montparnasse Tower changed the skyline, the district is still popular for its brasseries and cinemas.

Beyond the Centre. Heterogenous, outlying Paris includes villagey Charonne, smart Auteuil and urban renewal in Chinatown and at La Villette. Parisians tend to be disdainful of the suburbs, but nearby St-Denis, Vincennes and St-Cloud all have royal connections; attractions range from a castle to a football stadium; and there are signs that Paris is beginning to look beyond its frontiers and envisage the creation of a Grand Paris.

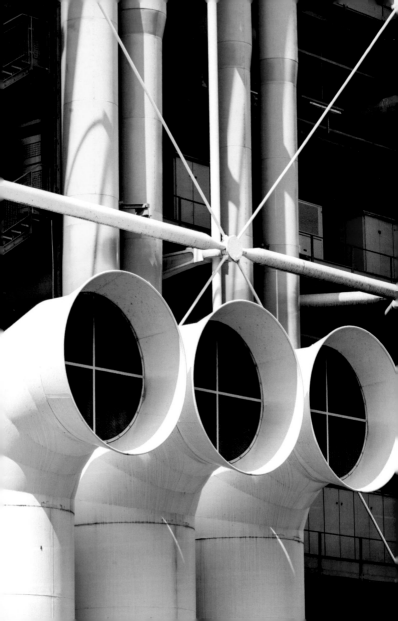

THE ISLANDS AND THE MARAIS

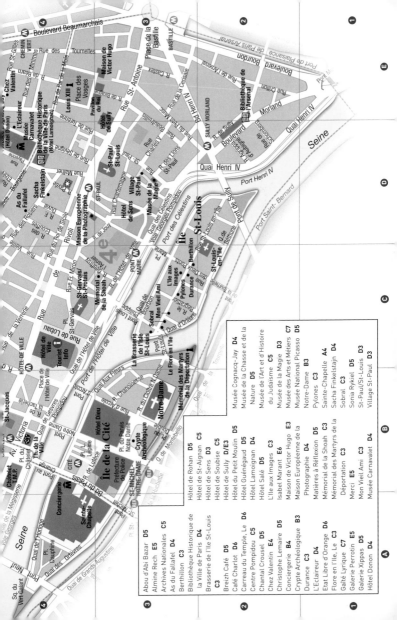

Eyeball the medieval gargoyles at Notre-Dame

Climbing the spiral staircase up the north tower of *Notre-Dame* and emerging onto the gallery high up on the west front, eye to eye with the gargoyles and chimeras, there is probably no better place to reflect on the skill of the medieval stonemason and the faith that made this one of France's great Gothic cathedrals. An additional hike takes you up the south tower past the giant 17th-century bourdon bell, Emmanuel, and onto the roof itself, to be met by the view immortalised in the brilliant 1939 film version of Victor Hugo's *The Hunchback of Notre-Dame* – where Charles Laughton scuttles across

the rooftop as Quasimodo. In fact, the original French title of the book is *Notre-Dame de Paris*, which suggests that the true hero of the tale is the cathedral itself. Hugo was passionate about the monument, though he complained about its decrepit, mutilated state and campaigned for its restoration.

Restoration eventually began in the 1840s by fervent Gothic Revivalist Eugène Viollet-le-Duc. Some of his chimeras are no doubt too Gothic to be true but the works did save the cathedral, famed – despite a rather gloomy interior – for its three richly carved portals, its rose windows and massive flying buttresses.

This is Paris's most visited monument, and yet still very much a place of worship: used for services – including a memorial service for the victims of the 2015 terrorist attacks – and organ recitals, state funerals and a vast procession for August's Fête de l'Assomption.

Cathédrale Notre-Dame de Paris; parvis de Notre-Dame; tel: 01 42 34 56 10; towers tel: 01 53 10 07 00; www.notredamede paris.fr; Mon–Fri 8am-6.45pm, Sat-Sun 8am-7.15pm, towers Apr–Sept daily 10am-6.30pm, May-Aug until 11pm Sat-Sun, Oct–Mar daily 10am-5.30pm; free, charge for towers; map B3

Read stained-glass stories at the Sainte-Chapelle

When Louis IX purchased the Crown of Thorns and some fragments of the True Cross from the impoverished Emperor Baldwin II in Constantinople, for 135,000 livres in 1239, he instantly boosted his prestige and saintly reputation as well as that of Paris. The king then set about building a suitably magnificent receptacle for his precious relics, erecting the double-decker Sainte Chapelle in record speed between 1242 and 1248 in the heart of the royal palace.

A gem of Flamboyant Gothic architecture, the chapel is all the more jewel-like for being hidden from the street within the Palais de Justice, Paris's central law courts, so that you often encounter two queues snaking along – one for the chapel and one for those waiting to sit in on trials.

Between the chapel's two levels, a striking contrast operates. The lower chapel, originally for the use of palace servants, is dark and intimate, with an early fresco of the Annunciation and its vaulted ceiling painted with fleur de lys against the blue of a night sky. Conversely, arrive in the upper chapel, once reserved for the royal family and clergy, and you are thrown into the light glinting off pale stone and the dappled reflections, all deep blues and ruby reds, from

the stained glass windows that seem to take up almost all of the chapel's upper section. In a jigsaw of small intensely coloured pieces, most of its original, minuscule figures depict 1,113 scenes from the Old Testament and the Crucifixion, to be read from the bottom up, while one window recounts the story of the relics themselves.

Sainte Chapelle; 4 boulevard du Palais; tel: 01 53 40 60 80; http://sainte-chapelle. monuments-nationaux.fr; Mar–Oct daily 9.30am–6pm, (15 May–15 Sept Wed until 9pm), Nov–Feb daily 9am–5pm; charge, bring ID; map A4

Feel the fear in the cells of the condemned at the Conciergerie, Marie-Antoinette's last dwelling place

When the royals took up residence at Vincennes and the Louvre, the palace became a prison under the control of the Concierge; the second part of the visit reflects this gory episode. During the Revolution, hundreds passed by here on their way to the guillotine, condemned by the Tribunal Révolutionnaire whose members included the revolutionary Robespierre – who himself fell victim to the Terror in 1794.

A handful of the cells have been re-created to show how conditions varied according to status or income: from the *paillasse*, the communal area where poorer prisoners slept on *paille* (straw) on the floor, via the *pistole* for those who could pay for beds, to the cells of the privileged or wealthy, kitted out with desks and lamps even. The probable location of the cell where Marie-Antoinette spent two months before execution now holds a chapel.

Exhibits include busts of Robespierre, keys, locks and a guillotine blade which hangs from the wall – understated but chilling.

Many people bypass the Conciergerie for the Sainte Chapelle – which is a pity, for the surprisingly extensive remains of the Capetian kings' medieval palace are a rare example of secular Gothic architecture and also one of the sights that best evokes the French Revolution.

Entry is directly into the Salle des Gens d'Armes, an impressive vaulted hall nearly 70 metres/yards long where a slab of black marble mounted on the wall is a remnant of one of the long tables used for banquets in the Great Hall above.

Conciergerie; 2 boulevard du Palais; tel: 01 53 40 60 80; http://conciergerie. monuments-nationaux.fr; daily 9.30am– 6pm; charge; map B4

Pay tribute to the past in the two crypts on Ile de la Cité

For an idea of what the Ile de la Cité was like before Baron Haussmann knocked down the clutter of medieval houses in front of Notre-Dame, descend into the **Crypte Archéologique** located under the parvis of the cathedral, an in-situ archaeological dig that takes you back centuries through the island's Roman and medieval past. There's a stretch of Roman quayside and bits of ramparts, the hypocaust from a bathing complex, medieval shop cellars, stairways, pavements, traces of a foundling hospital and a 19th-century sewer, all in a complicated layering which piled up as the ground level rose with all the debris.

At the other end of the cathedral, steps lead down to a very different sort of crypt: the **Mémorial des Martyrs de la Déportation**, a dignified monument to World War II deportees. Inaugurated in 1962, Georges-Henri Pingusson's architecture of iron bars and geometrical blocks of roughened white concrete is an ecumenical crypt in memory of all the Jews, Communists, homosexuals, gypsies and Resistance fighters who were deported from France. In the shrine you'll find fragments of glass recalling the thousands

of deportees, side galleries with triangular niches containing earth and cinders from the concentration camps, quotations from poems by Eluard, Aragon, Desnos, Sartre and Saint-Exupéry, and the inscription, 'forgive but don't forget'.

Crypte Archéologique; 7 parvis Notre-Dame; tel: 01 55 42 50 10; www.crypte. paris.fr; Tue–Sun 10am–6pm, last admission 5.30pm, charge; map B3 Mémorial des Martyrs de la Déportation; square de l'Ile de France; tel: 01 46 33 87 56; Apr–Sept daily 10am–7pm, Oct–Mar daily 10am–5pm; free; map C3

Stroll along a 17th-century high street on secluded Ile St-Louis

The picture of insular insouciance in the middle of the Seine, Ile St-Louis is a 17th-century timewarp that appears to have barely changed since it was created as a property venture between developer Christophe Marie and royal architect Louis Le Vau. Today, the island remains a highly desirable residential address and a lovely place for a stroll, its quais lined with elegant houses and bisected as it is by exclusive high street rue St-Louis-en-l'Ile. As on any self-respecting high street, here you'll find food shops (rather superior ones, of course) including a foie gras specialist, places to eat and tempting gift shops, most of

which are open on Sunday. Notable for their curiosity factor are the Hôtel du Jeu de Paume at No. 54, where rooms lead off a wood-framed *jeu de paume* (a precursor of tennis); and the leering dragons holding up the balcony of the Hôtel Chenizot, at No. 51 (during the week you can walk into the courtyard where there's another fine facade with sunburst motif).

The eastern section of the street is home to **Berthillon** (No. 31; tel: 01 43 54 31 61), Paris's most famous *glacier* (ice-cream shop). On the western side, temptations include Provençal soaps and perfumes at **Durance** (No. 37), chunky resin jewellery at **Sobral** (No. 79), gifts and gadgets at **Pylones** (No. 57) and historic and vintage photos and posters at **L'Ile aux Images** (No. 51). Stylish bistro **Mon Vieil Ami** (No. 69; tel: 01 40 46 01 35) is the most sophisticated place to eat, while flanking the Pont St-Louis – the footbridge leading to the Ile de la Cité – are Alsatian stalwart **La Brasserie de l'Isle St-Louis** (tel: 01 43 54 02 59), and tearoom-cum-café **Le Flore en l'Ile** (tel: 01 43 29 88 27), renowned for its rich hot chocolate far too thick to pour.

Ile St-Louis; map C3–D4

Discover sculptures and colonnades in the grand courtyards of the Marais

The Marais *hôtel particulier* (grand private townhouse) was the des res of 17th-century nobles and civil servants who needed to be in town near the royal court, typically in a fine house set behind an entrance courtyard, with wings, the requisite stabling and formal gardens at the rear. When the Marais fell from fashion the houses became industrial premises and tenements, but many have now been beautifully restored. Several are museums, including **Hôtel Carnavalet** (see page 35), **Hôtel Guénégaud** (see page 37), **Hôtel de St-Aignan** (see page 38), **Hôtel Donon** (Musée Cognacq-Jay, 8 rue Elzévir; map D4), and **Hôtel Salé** (map D5), now the Picasso Museum (5 rue Thorigny; www.musee-picasso.fr). Others house galleries, shops, schools, even the fire station on rue de Sévigné. Everywhere, you can spot fine doorways and carved heads, and during the week, you can often wander into its courtyards.

Cross through the **Hôtel de Sully** (map D/E3) between 62 rue St-Antoine and the place des Vosges to admire sculpted facades representing the elements and the seasons. **Hôtel Lamoignan** (24 rue Pavée; map D4), now the Paris history library but built in the 1580s for Diane

de France, daughter of Henri II, has a Renaissance courtyard with giant order pilasters and Greek key motifs. On rue des Francs-Bourgeois, lined with numerous 17th- and 18th-century mansions, the **Hôtel de Soubise** (No. 60; tel: 01 40 27 60 96; map C5), now the National Archives, has a glorious colonnaded *cour d'honneur* (main courtyard; pictured). The real treat here, however, are its grand rococo interiors decorated in the 1730s by Van Loo, Lemoyne, Restout and Natoire for the Prince de Soubise; the Salon du Prince is used for concerts, while its restored gardens connect to the **Hôtel de Rohan** (map D5), built for one of the prince's sons and famed for its relief *The Stallions of the Sun*.

Drop in on Victor Hugo at his very personal apartment on place des Vosges

Henri IV had plenty of town planning schemes for Paris, and in 1605, with the glorious arcaded **place des Vosges** (originally place Royale), he got it just right: a symmetrical square with 34 identical pavilions punctuated by the Pavillon de la Reine on one side and the Pavillon du Roi on the other. Its Flemish Renaissance-influenced style has been attributed to the Métezeau brothers, who designed the remarkably similar place Ducale in Charleville-Mezières. In fact the pavilions in red brick with stone chaining and steep slate roofs are just a facade – look closely and you'll see that on some the brick is imitation – and plots of various sizes were sold off behind to assorted royal officials and entrepreneurs. As for the gardens in the centre, they were created in the 1630s complete with an equestrian statue of Louis XIII, though the railings, trees, fountains and playgrounds came later on.

Victor Hugo had the good fortune to live on the square when he, along with his wife and four children, rented an apartment on the second floor of the Hôtel de Rohan-Guéménée, now the **Maison de Victor Hugo**, from 1832 to 1848. Here he would write many of his poems and sever-

al novels, including *Marie Tudor* and *Ruy Blas*. A series of rooms evokes different periods of his life and his numerous passions, including the eccentric pseudo-medieval dining room furniture he designed for long-standing mistress Juliette Drouet when in exile in Guernsey

(after opposing Napoleon III's coup d'état), and his enthusiasm for the newfangled art of photography.

Maison de Victor Hugo; 6 place des Vosges; tel: 01 42 72 10 16; www.maisons victorhugo.paris.fr; Tue–Sun 10am–6pm; free; map E3

Musée Carnavalet closure

Paris's history museum (23 rue de Sévigné) will be closed from October 2016 until 2019 – though you will still be able to see its beautifully land-scaped courtyard. The renovation will give a new lease of life to a once confusing but fascinating museum.

Ride the iconic escalators at powerhouse for modern art and architecture the Centre Pompidou

A fabulous intrusion in the Parisian cityscape, the **Centre Pompidou** – named after French president Georges Pompidou (1911–74) – catapulted architects Richard Rogers and Renzo Piano to fame; more than 30 years after opening, it's still one of the most exciting buildings in Paris and a savvy extension of the urban environment. Going for the boiler house look meant that all service conduits and escalators were located on the outside, leaving the inside free for moveable walls. Crucially, this was also a boiler house of interaction, setting a pluridisciplinary model that has since been aped the world over. The airy central forum leads to an art museum, exhibition galleries, auditoria, cinema, reference library and experimental music institute. There are special galleries for children and teenagers and a full cultural programme on offer.

The permanent collection of the **Musée National d'Art Moderne** gives an unrivalled picture of the history of modern art from 1906 to the present, from Fauvism to multimedia. Only a fragment of the collection is shown at a time; but on the fifth floor in the historical section, you can be sure to find Picasso, Braque and the Cubists, superb works by Matisse, the birth of abstraction with Kandinsky and the Delaunays, Malevich, one-off individuals like Rouault or Francis Bacon, Dada including Duchamp's iconic *Fountain*, Surrealist paintings, and the wall from André Breton's apartment with his collection of tribal art.

On the floor below it's Pop and *nouveau réalisme*, arte povera and conceptual art, video art and installations, Warhol's *Ten Lizzes* or a giant mushroom by Carsten Holler. Big prestigious exhibitions are held on the sixth floor, next to the slinky aluminium pods of restaurant Georges, great anytime or a buzzy nightime destination for people-watching with a view.

Centre Pompidou; tel: 01 44 78 33 12; www.centrepompidou.fr; Wed–Mon 11am–9pm; charge; map C5

Track down a bestiary at the Musée de la Chasse et de la Nature

On the same premises as an aristocratic hunting club, this eccentric museum dedicated to nature and the hunt has been imaginatively renovated in the beautiful Hôtel de Guénégaud (designed by François Mansart in 1651–55 for the king's secretary, Jean-François Guénégaud des Brosses) and the adjacent Hôtel de Mongelas (1705). This is an intriguing museum if only because gauging where it stands – somewhere between animal lover and fervent hunter, as seen out in the autumnal French countryside – can be quite tricky. But that's part of the point: this is an exploration of the image of the wild animal, man's relation to nature, and the inspiration animals have given to the fine and decorative arts.

Much of the museum is arranged roughly by species, with rooms dedicated to wild boar, deer, dogs, wolves and even a cabinet of curiosities on the mythical unicorn. Slightly scary stuffed tigers and a massive rampant bear inhabit one room; another is full of beautifully crafted shotguns, bows and spears. There are old masters by Cranach and Snyders, painted porcelain tea services and animal-shaped porcelain tureens, and a large collection of Desportes' vivid oil sketches of animals, as well as his portrait of Diane and Blond, Louis XIV's favourite hunting dogs. The museum has also integrated works by contemporary artists, including photos by Eric Poitevin, a Jeff Koons' porcelain *Puppy* and, in a tiny panelled room containing two panels by Rubens and Velvet Brueghel, a mysterious owl feather ceiling by Belgian artist Jan Fabre – where beady eyes stare down at you from above.

Musée de la Chasse et de la Nature; 62 rue des Archives; tel: 01 53 01 92 40; www.chassenature.org; Tue–Sun 11am–6pm; charge; map D5

Choose between cheesecake and falafel in the Jewish Marais

If the Marais' Jewish community, the *pletzl*, originally largely consisted of Ashkenazy Jews – first from Alsace after the emancipation brought by the Revolution, later fleeing the pogroms in Eastern Europe at the end of the 19th century – more recently it has been joined by Sephardic Jews from North Africa following the end of French colonisation. This cosmopolitan mix of origins is satisfyingly summed up in rue des Rosiers, where the traditional bakers, delis and Judaica shops of central Europe mingle with North African falafel joints, amid the ever-encroaching fashion boutiques. Try **Sacha Finkelstajn** (No. 27; tel: 01 42 72 78 91) for plaited hallah bread, poppyseed cake, excellent cheesecake, strudel, *perojskis*, dill peppers and hot salt beef sandwiches; and the **As du Fallafel** (No. 34; tel: 01 48 87 63 60) for spicy tahini-laden falafel to take away or eat at a handful of tables. Around the corner, the synagogue at 10 rue Pavée was designed in 1913 by Hector Guimard, better known for his Art Nouveau metro entrances.

At the **Musée d'Art et d'Histoire du Judaïsme**, Jewish history is treated not only as a history of diasporas and religious ceremonies, but as a history of art and the decorative arts too. Displayed in the beautifully restored 17th-century Hôtel de Saint-Aignan, the collection includes torah scrolls and hannukah lamps, artefacts from the printing tradition along with fabulous Baroque silverware from Holland, and ornate costumes and jewellery from North Africa and Turkey. After dealing with Jewish communities and traditions around the world, the gallery turns its focus onto Jews in France after the Revolution, the Dreyfus case, intellectual life and an impressive array of paintings and sculptures by Jewish artists of the Ecole de Paris – such as Chagall, Modigliani, Lipchitz and Chana Orloff. The museum deliberately does not cover the Holocaust, although a work by artist Christian Boltanski in a narrow courtyard recalls the numerous Jewish families who were living in flats in this very building in 1939.

Instead, the Holocaust is remembered at the **Mémorial de la Shoah**. Enter past the Wall of Names, the list of 76,000 Jews deported from France of whom only about 2,500 survived, despite the best efforts of the *justes* who hid and helped Jews in France during the war – more than 2,000 *justes* are listed on an external wall along the Allée des Justes. Inside is a crypt containing the Memorial to the Unknown Jewish Martyr, with an eternal flame burning at the centre of a marble star of David and a room of chillingly meticulous police files kept by the Vichy regime. The memorial was extended in 2005 with a sober but not melodramatic presentation of the history of the deportations and concentration camps in France and the rest of Europe. Photographs, letters, newspaper clippings and film interviews of survivors highlight personal stories against the broad current of events, ending with a moving wall of photos of France's 3,000 child deportees.

Musée d'Art et d'Histoire du Judaisme; 71 rue du Temple; tel: 01 53 01 86 60; www.mahj.org; Mon–Fri 11am–6pm, Sun 10am–6pm; charge; map C5
Mémorial de la Shoah; 17 rue Geoffroy l'Asnier; tel: 01 42 77 44 72; www.memorial delashoah.org; Sun–Fri 10am–6pm, Thur until 10pm; free; map C3

Browse in the junk shops of Village St-Paul, a labyrinth of tucked-away courtyards

Between rue St-Antoine and the river sits St-Paul, a less frenzied district away from the hype and continual fashion parade of the northern Marais. **Eglise St-Paul** (99 rue St-Antoine) is a Counter-Reformation church modelled on the Gesù in Rome with an impressive skylit dome; exit from a side door and an alley leads to rue St-Paul. Follow the road down to a series of archways through which lies the labyrinth of interconnected courtyards of the **Village St-Paul**, home to antiques dealers and *brocanteurs*, where eclectic wares run from vintage furniture to wine gadgets. A handful of cafés and bistros include **Cru**, for raw food buffs, whilst on rue des Jardins-St-Paul, the

longest visible section of Philippe Augustus's city wall, built in 1190 complete with a watchtower, runs down the side of a sports ground.

Back on rue St-Paul is the discreet entrance of the **Musée de la Magie**, prized by children and prestidigitators. Distorting mirrors, optical illusions and a couple of trunks for cutting ladies in half are displayed around vaulted cellars. Visits include a magic show.

While in the area take a look at the melodramatically turreted **Hôtel de Sens** (1 rue Figuier; www.paris.fr); along with the Hôtel de Cluny, this rare surviving Gothic mansion is a precursor of the Marais *hôtel particulier* (see page 33). Nearby, the **Maison Européenne de la Photographie** is a great photography space and its minimalist modern extension, with frequently changing shows of historic and contemporary photography, features an unusual collection of Polaroids.

Musée de la Magie; 11 rue St-Paul; tel: 01 42 72 13 26; www.museedelamagie.com; Wed, Sat, Sun 2–7pm; charge; map D3
Maison Européenne de la Photographie, 5 rue de Fourcy; tel: 01 44 78 75 00; www.3mep-fr.org; Wed–Sun 11am–7.45pm; charge; map D4

Gallery hop on rue de Turenne and rue Vieille-du-Temple

If there's one thing you can be sure of, it's that the art world will turn out for a *vernissage* (private view) at the dynamic **Galerie Perrotin** (76 rue de Turenne; tel: 01 42 16 79 79; www. perrotin.com; map E5), one of the city's most happening art galleries. Here you can expect big showy pieces from a trendy international list studded with the likes of Takashi Murakami, Maurizio Cattelan and Bharti Kher, and French artists Sophie Calle, Xavier Veilhan and Kolkoz. Emmanuel Perrotin began showing artists in his flat twenty years ago. He now occupies three floors of a Marais mansion, an adjacent industrial brick building and another gallery across the street behind. Around the corner, **Galerie Xippas** (108 rue Vieille-du-Temple; tel: 01 40 27 05 55; www.xippas. com; map D5), founded in Paris in 1990 but now also with showrooms in Switzerland and Uruguay, is one of the leading and largest galleries in Paris dedicated to upcoming and established contemporary artists; the basement is a showroom while upstairs is the exhibition space. Another must on the art circuit is **Chantal Crousel** (10 rue Charlot; tel: 01 42 77 38 87; www.crousel.com; map D5; pictured) for interesting installation and video art from artists

including Mona Hatoum, Thomas Hirschhorn, Anri Sala or Rirkrit Tiravanija – who constructed an entire wooden barge here. At **Chez Valentin** (9 rue St-Gilles; tel: 01 48 87 42 55; www.galeriechezvalentin. com; map E4) shows tend to be complex and conceptual; while **Almine Rech** (64 rue de Turenne; tel: 01 45 83 71 90; www.alminerech. com; map D5) shows painters and photographers, often with minimalist tendencies, around the whitewashed rooms of an old house.

To see what shows are on or coming up, pick up the *Galeries mode d'emploi* leaflet in one of the galleries or check out www. fondation-entreprise-ricard.com and www.paris-art.com.

Hang out with the fashionistas in the Haut-Marais

With its one-off boutiques and quirky mix of hip labels, vintage discoveries and rising designers, the Haut-Marais (map D4–5, E5–6) has become an essential destination for the fashion pack. Entered through a period doorway, **L'Eclaireur** (40 rue de Sévigné; tel: 01 48 87 10 22; www.leclaireur.com) is worth a look as much for the extraordinary interior of cascading planks and flickering video screens by Belgian artist-architect Arne Quinze as for its hip selection of luxury womenswear and bags by Céline, Balenciaga or Marni. However, the real hub for those on the fashion trail is to be found around the junction of rue Vieille-du-Temple and rue de Poitou: check out the women's fashion selection at **Abou d'Abi Bazar** (125 rue Vieille-du-Temple; tel: 01 42 71 13 26; www.aboudabi bazar.com). As well as the **Hôtel du Petit Moulin** (29 rue de Poitou; tel: 01 42 74 10 10; www.hotelpetit moulinparis.com) – the first hotel designed by fashion maestro Christian Lacroix – rue de Poitou has a throng of interesting outlets, such as **Matières à Réflexion** at No. 19 (tel: 01 42 72 16 31; www.matieres areflexion.com), which brings together the trends for vintage and recycling, where old leather jackets are turned into characterful handbags – you can even take in your own beloved leather jacket for a customised version. The window displays are always particularly good at **Christophe Lemaire** (No. 28; tel: 01 44 78 00 09; www. lemaire.fr), a boutique set in an old corner pharmacy, where Lemaire, the former womenswear designer for Hermès, shows off his own flowing Japanese-influenced men's and women's lines. French fashion legend **Sonia Rykiel** recently opened a store here (No. 37; tel: 01 84 83 03 30; www.soniarykiel.com). Also, don't miss **Isabel Marant** (47 rue de Saintonge; tel: 01 42 78 19 24; www. isabelmarant.com) either for her quirky yet wearable threads with a neo-hippie look and ethnic touches.

Fashionistas take a breather and refreshments at trendy **Café Charlot** (38 rue de Bretagne; tel: 01 44 54 03 30; www.cafecharlotparis. com), housed in a former bakery and a favourite of Oscar-winning actor Jean Dujardin, or tuck into sweet and savoury pancakes in the beach shack setting of Paris's most fashionable crêperie, **Breizh Café** (109 rue Vieille-du-Temple; tel: 01 42 72 13 77; www.breizhcafe.com). Tying all the strands together is **Merci** (111 boulevard Beaumarchais; tel: 01 42 77 00 33; www. merci-merci.com): three storeys of artfully distressed industrial space where you'll find a brilliantly eclectic choice of new and pre-owned clothes, furniture, kitchen items, hardware, perfumes and light switches. You can stop for lunch downstairs or sip a coffee in Merci's café-cum-secondhand-bookstore (pictured). The latest addition to the area is the **Carreau du Temple** (4 rue Eugène Spuller; tel: 01 83 81 93 30; www.carreaudutemple.eu), once a covered market, and since 2014 a multi-use public space hosting everything from aerobics classes to fashion shows for big names like Saint Laurent; it also puts on a wide range of cultural activities and provides studio space for artists.

Lose yourself in electronic soundscapes at the digitally daring Gaîté Lyrique

An ornate 19th-century facade of red marble and grandiose columns hides the **Gaîté Lyrique**, reborn as a daring new cultural centre with a mission to bring you all that is up to the minute in electronic arts and digital technology. The building itself has had a chequered history, from its glorious origins as the theatre where some of Offenbach's operettas were first performed to an ill-fated attempt to turn it into a theme park in the 1980s, when most of the old interior was ripped out. Only the grand foyer, now hung with flying-saucer lights and concealed speakers, remains from 1862, leaving a concrete shell for seven storeys of auditoria, galleries, cafés, a boutique, and rehearsal and recording studios. You'll notice colourful modules that can be perambulated around the building and serve as everything from individual video-screening booths to offices and cloakrooms; as well as white polyhedric blocks that can be assembled into seats, bars and information counters, or illuminated as lamps. The Gaîté Lyrique has an admirably broad vision of digital culture, a desire to make it accessible to everyone and an international approach. Since its opening in 2011, it has invited artists and photographers, musicians and skateboarders – this one-time theatre is turning out to be a surprisingly apt setting for a decidedly theatrical approach. The Gaîté's programme includes not only concerts but debates and brunches, performance and DJs, a padded booth for listening to electronic soundworks, a computer gaming room, and art installations that react as you walk past them.

Gaîté Lyrique; 3 bis rue Papin; tel: 01 53 01 51 51; www.gaite-lyrique.net; Tue–Sat 2–8pm, Sun noon–6pm, concert times vary; map C7

Tune into technology at the Musée des Arts et Métiers

Unlike the pure-science emphasis adopted by Paris's other science museums, the unusual **Musée des Arts et Métiers** is more about engineering and inventions, set amid the striking architecture of the medieval priory of Saint-Martin-des-Champs. The museum was founded in 1794 by the Abbé Grégoire, a member of the Revolutionary Convention, to train engineers and technicians; the rails by which pieces of apparatus were trundled off to lecture halls for demonstration are still visible in the parquet flooring. There are sections devoted to mechanics and materials, construction and communications, from astrolabes and Pascal's calculator to TVs, computers and a 1960's jukebox, not to mention a collection of elaborate 18th-century musical automatons. Most spectacular of the displays is undoubtedly the cars and aeroplanes in the nave, including the plane in which Louis Blériot made the first flight across the Channel in 1909. Some of the most memorable items, however, are those inventions that didn't quite work, such as Clément Ader's fragile bat-like plane that hangs in the grand stairway, flying rather more successfully now than when it hopped along the ground in 1890. Keeping up the steam theme is a good café, A Toutes Vapeurs, specialising in steamed dishes.

Musée des Arts et Métiers; 60 rue Réaumur; tel: 01 53 01 82 00; www.arts-et-metiers.net; Tue–Sun 10am–6pm, Thur until 9.30pm; charge; map C7

LOUVRE, OPÉRA AND GRANDS BOULEVARDS

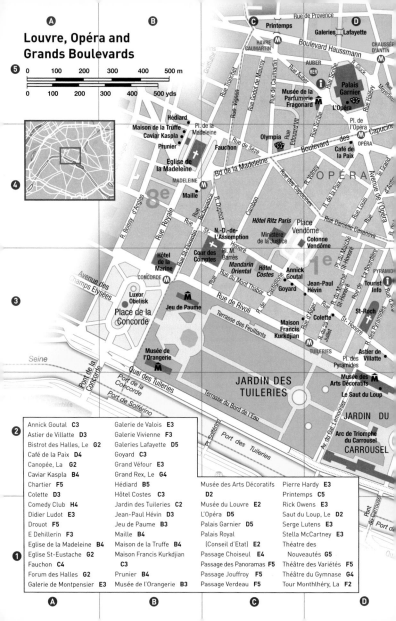

Louvre, Opéra and Grands Boulevards

Rue de Provence

Printemps

Galeries Lafayette

Rue de Mogador

Boulevard Haussmann

HAVRE CAUMARTIN

CHAUSSÉE D'ANTIN

AUBER

Palais Garnier

Musée de la Parfumerie Fragonard

L'Opéra

Pl. de l'Opéra

Hédiard

Maison de la Truffe

Caviar Kaspla

Pl. de la Madeleine

Prunier

Fauchon

Olympia

Rue de Sèze

Café de la Paix

Église de la Madeleine

Bd de la Madeleine

MADELEINE

OPÉRA

Maille

Avenue de l'Opéra

N.-D.-de-L'Assomption

Hôtel Ritz Paris

Place Vendôme

Rue Danielle Casanova

Ministère de la Justice

Colonne Vendôme

Hôtel de la Marine

Cour des Comptes

Mandarin Oriental

Hôtel Costes

Annick Goutal

Jean-Paul Hévin

Tourist Info

CONCORDE

Rue du Mont Thabor

Goyard

PYRAMIDE

Luxor Obelisk

Place de la Concorde

Jeu de Paume

Rue de Rivoli

Colette

St-Roch

Maison Francis Kurkdjian

Terrasse des Feuillants

Astier de Villatte

Musée de l'Orangerie

Pl. des Pyramides

Musée des Arts Décoratifs

Seine

Quai des Tuileries

JARDIN DES TUILERIES

Le Saut du Loup

Pont de la Concorde

Port de la Concorde

Port de Solférino

Terrasse du Bord de l'Eau

JARDIN DU

Pont de Solférino

Port des Tuileries

Arc de Triomphe du Carrousel

CARROUSEL

Pick a side in the battle of Romantics versus Classicists at the Louvre

Pitting the two rival tendencies in late 18th and early 19th century painting – neoclassicists and romantics, line versus colour – the Grande Galerie sums up French art in all its grandeur. A period when French artists were impassioned observers or even participants in current events (with an eye for dressing things up in mythology), it's a perfect preview before tackling the rest of the museum. On one side, you'll find the political neoclassicism of David's *Oath of the Horatii* and *Sacre de Napoléon*, where the emperor is crowned in Notre-Dame before a cast of millions. While across the hallway comes the flamboyance, emotion, motion and colour of Romanticism: Delacroix's *Liberty Leading the People*, where the tricolore-bearing figure of Marianne is as much a bravura manifesto as a depiction of the Revolution, and his delightfully daft and bloodthirsty *Death of Sardanapalus*.

As the world's largest museum, you could spend months here, and even though the throng often almost blocks the view of the *Mona Lisa*, take a small staircase and you can suddenly find yourself alone. So, allow yourself to get a little lost to make your own discoveries: unlikely attics with battle scenes by Charles Le Brun, Rubens' vast cycle of the *Life of Marie de Médicis* that contrasts with two sparkling, loving portraits of his wife, or small rooms containing gems of northern painting such as Vermeer's *The Lacemaker*. For all its size, the Louvre is surprisingly user-friendly, though be sure to pick up a map in the entrance hall.

Musée du Louvre; rue de Rivoli; tel: 01 40 20 50 50; www.louvre.fr, Wed–Mon 9am–6pm, Wed and Fri until 9.45pm; charge; map E2

50

Shop where revolutionaries once plotted in the arcades around Palais-Royal

For evidence of how even the most historic-looking districts are continually being reinvented, you only have to visit the arcades surrounding the Palais-Royal gardens. What had been a sleepy backwater selling musical boxes and medals has shot into the superleague of adventurous fashion. Almost side by side on **Galerie de Valois** are **Pierre Hardy** (No. 156), for streetwise yet intellectual men's and women's shoes (think Mondrian on feet); the arty/distressed look of **Rick Owens** (No. 130–133); and the huge **Stella McCartney** store (No. 114–121). Galerie Montpensier has **Didier Ludot** (No. 24), guru of vintage fashion.

Just the rustle of shopping bags disturbs the calm of the gardens, a lovely oasis in the heart of Paris. While the palace itself (now the Conseil d'Etat and Ministry of Culture) was built in the 1630s for Cardinal Richelieu, the galleries were added in the 18th century, becoming a place where high life met low life in gambling dens and cafés. At Café de Foy, Camille Desmoulins called upon his comrades to storm the Bastille prison on 13 July 1789, marking the start of the Revolution. The Café de Chartres, opened in 1784, is now the splendid **Grand Véfour** (17 rue de Beaujolais; tel: 01 42 96 56 27; www.

grand-vefour.com) with fine cuisine, period interiors and its old name still visible on the facade.

Admire Daniel Buren's **black and white columns** in the palace courtyard. The artwork caused a stir when installed in 1986 but has become a favourite spot for sitting on, hopping on or dropping a coin.

Another curiosity is the midday cannon. Made by a clockmaker in 1786, it fired every day at noon, triggered by the sun passing the Paris *méridien*, allowing Parisians to set their watches. The original was stolen in 1998, but a replica goes off every Wednesday.

Palais-Royal; map E2–3

Gaze down through decades of interior design at the Musée des Arts Décoratifs

The top of the turret makes a good start to exploring the **Musée des Arts Décoratifs**: an astonishing view along rue de Rivoli out through bull's eye windows coupled with, internally, a visual descent through the decades of 20th-century design – from the 1940s on the 9th floor, via a pyramid of 1960s' chairs and very 1970s' sideboards, to the designers of today, such as Ron Arad, Gaetano Pesce and Philippe Starck.

Although it's located in a wing of the Louvre, the museum is independently run and the emphasis not on royal pieces. Instead, this place is all about French craftsmanship and design flair, tracking style trends and changing tastes over the centuries. Dotted around the collection are period rooms reconstructed whole, including Jeanne Lanvin's Art Deco suite, with its sultry blue boudoir and splendid marble bathroom. There's also a fabulous collection of jewellery, stunningly lit.

One side of the museum follows a chronological route, the other takes an interesting thematic approach, imaginatively mixing periods and bringing in items from the advertising and fashion museums also on the premises.

The museum has an excellent boutique, where you can find reproductions of historic dinner services. The smart modern restaurant, **Le Saut du Loup**, or 'wolf's leap', is named after the dry ditch that once ran along here as part of the Louvre's defenses.

Musée des Arts Décoratifs; 107 rue de Rivoli; tel: 01 44 55 57 50; www.lesarts decoratifs.fr; Tue–Sun 11am–6pm; charge; map D2

Surrender your senses to designer scents by Serge Lutens, Francis Kurkdjian and Annick Goutal

Perfume is a rarefied experience at the boutique of **Serge Lutens** (142 Galerie de Vallois, Jardins du Palais-Royal; tel: 01 49 27 09 09; www.sergelutens.com; map E3), where you are led into an exquisite, purple-panelled boudoir to discover intense, sensual perfumes, presented in pretty bell-jar bottles.

At the pristine white and zinc **Maison Francis Kurkdjian** (5 rue d'Alger; tel: 01 42 60 07 07; www.franciskurkdjian.com; map C3), near the Jardin des Tuileries, Francis Kurkdjian takes a far more iconoclastic approach. He can create exclusive bespoke perfumes, but wants fragrance to be part of everyday life. Here you'll find not only men's and women's perfumes but also scented washing liquid and tubes of pear, herb, mint or violet liquid for blowing bubbles – meant for kids, adored by parents.

North of the Tuileries, **Annick Goutal** (14 rue de Castiligione; tel: 01 42 60 52 82; www.annickgoutal.com; map C3) is classic and elegant. Staff will take you through the 40 or so perfumes and aftershaves, including bestseller Eau d'Hadrien, all made from natural ingredients. Inspired by the South of France or North Africa, the range extends to home fragrances and luxury skin products.

Other specialist perfumeries

Détaille (10 rue St-Lazare; tel: 01 48 78 68 50; www.detaille.com; map page 82 E2): just as it was when founded in 1905, with evocative colognes called Aéroplane, Yachting or Escrimeur.

Diptyque (34 boulevard St-Germain; tel: 01 43 26 77 44; www.diptyque paris.fr; map page 112 E4): for legendary room candles.

Editions du Parfum Frédéric Malle (37 rue de Grenelle; tel: 01 42 22 76 40; www.fredericmalle.com; map page 130 D5): scents by famous noses and glass booths for sniffing them in.

Etat Libre d'Orange (69 rue des Archives; tel: 01 42 78 30 09; https://etatlibredorange.com; map page 26 D6): cheerfully irreverent, great scents with silly names.

Guerlain (68 av des Champs-Elysées; tel: 01 45 62 52 57; www.guerlain.com; map page 66 E4): the Belle Epoque home of *Shalimar*, plus a beauty salon.

Nose out next year's fashion and lifestyle trends on rue St-Honoré

Dignified rue St-Honoré (map C3-D3) has been a must for the dedicated shopper ever since pioneering concept store **Colette** (213 rue St-Honoré; www.colette.fr) opened in 1998, conveniently close for the fashion and film set at black-fronted **Hôtel Costes** (No. 239; tel: 01 42 44 50 00; www.hotelcostes.com) up the street. The white, minimalist, multi-level boutique takes the bazaar-like ethos of the department store and pares it down to a cutting-edge *what's next* in fashion, electronic gadgets, style magazines, make up, household objects and even toys. A decade on, it remains resolutely cool yet eclectic enough to spring a few surprises.

Okay, you wouldn't want to own everything here; and some of the limited-edition trainers are absurdly expensive, strictly for the cognoscenti. But Colette has proved to have its finger on the pulse, the first to highlight some bright young designers such as Olympia Le Tan, with her clever little handbags made from classic book covers.

The mezzanine level exhibits hip photographers and graphic designers, while the basement bar is a fashionable lunch spot, specialising in... well, water, mineral waters from all over the globe to be precise.

The arrival of Colette prompted a stream of French and Italian fashion labels to follow, including Roberto Cavalli, Miu Miu, Paule Ka, MaxMara, Jacques Le Corre's hats, and the chic-yet-affordable Sandro and Maje. At No. 173, the seductively wonky, glazed white earthenware teapots and dinner services of **Astier de Villatte** (tel: 01 42 60 74 13) evoke the shabby-chic château lifestyle of a lost aristocratic past. A true survivor is **Goyard** at No. 233, maker of luxury fitted trunks and luggage since 1825. And if you don't want water chez Colette, master *chocolatier* **Jean-Paul Hévin** (No. 231) has a cocoa-coloured Chocolate Bar tucked upstairs, for indulging in gâteaux and hot chocolate.

Switch from funfairs to Monet's waterlilies all in the space of the Tuileries gardens

If variety is the spice of life, then the Tuileries gardens do pretty well. The park was originally laid out by Louis XIV's master gardener, André Le Nôtre, as part of the royal master-plan, stretching between the Louvre and the Tuileries palace on the site of an old tile (*tuile*) factory. At first sight, it looks very much the classic French park with long gravel paths, clipped geometric trees and white marble statuary; but it also has kids' trampolines, a funky vegetable garden, and a line of cafés down the central axis.

The park makes for a good rest stop while visiting the Louvre but actually, can lay claim to plenty of art of its own. In the Jardin du Carrousel, near the Louvre, statues by Aristide Maillol hide between little hedges. Towards place de la Concorde, the **Jeu de Paume**, once a real tennis court, is used for photography exhibitions. The **Musée de l'Orangerie** provides the setting for Monet's fabulous later paintings of waterlilies. Two specially conceived oval rooms with softly filtered daylight allows you to appreciate the large curved canvases (the longest is 17 metres/yds long) of his water garden at Giverny, painted in different seasons and at different times of day between 1914 and 1926 and verging on abstraction. In the basement are Impressionist and post-Impressionist paintings collected by art dealer Paul Guillaume, notably Cézanne still lifes, early Matisse, and works by Soutine and Henri Rousseau.

Jeu de Paume; 1 place de la Concorde; tel: 01 47 03 12 50; www.jeudepaume.org; Tue 11am–9pm, Wed–Sun 11am–7pm; charge; map B3
Musée de l'Orangerie; Jardin des Tuileries; tel: 01 44 77 80 07; www.musee-orangerie. fr; Wed–Mon 9am–6pm; charge; map B3

Find traces of Paris's market past at Les Halles

For centuries Les Halles was the market heart, or perhaps belly, of Paris. It lost its soul when the whole-sale market moved out of town in 1969 and the green metal pavilions were knocked down. The Forum des Halles (map G2) shopping centre and transport intersection that replaced it was largely a place to avoid – so no-one wept its demolition in 2010 to be replaced by an ambitious shop-ping and entertainment complex complete with a new, undulating roof, **La Canopée**, and vast garden land-scaped into various themed areas. The Forum reopened in 2016; the garden is due for completion in 2018.

Traces of the area's lively market past do linger in the all-night res-taurants that once fed market work-ers at all hours, and in the kitchen emporiums – such as **E Dehillerin** (18–20 rue Coquillière; tel: 01 42 36 53 13; www.e-dehillerin.fr; map F3),

supplying chefs and keen amateur cooks for nearly two centuries.

South of the gardens, **La Tour Monthlhéry** (5 rue des Prouvaires; tel: 01 45 36 21 82; closed at week-ends; map F2), aka Chez Denise, serves huge steaks and piles of lamb chops until 5am. It's dead trad and very popular with visitors, while **Le Bistrot des Halles** (15 rue des Halles; tel: 01 42 36 91 69; map G2), with its plate glass and formica, is a pleasantly un-dressed up spot for good, solid food and wines by the glass that is busy at lunchtime.

The end of the market is depicted in a charming relief, *The Departure of the Fruits and Vegetables from the Heart of Paris, 28 February 1969* by Raymond Mason inside **Eglise St-Eustache** (map G2), long the market church (also known for its impressive organ, with free recitals every Sunday at 5.30pm).

Bask in romance and splendour at the Palais Garnier

It's hard to imagine anything more extravagant than the **Palais Garnier**, the opera house that has come to symbolise Second Empire Paris and Napoleon III's ambition to make Paris the most beautiful city in the world, and which is still an incredibly glamorous place to watch opera or the ballet. It was built between 1860 and 1875, after Charles Garnier saw off 170 competing architects, concocting a gloriously eclectic affair. If you don't have tickets for a performance, visit during the day to absorb the fabulously over-the-top decor. For visits, the entrance is at the side, beneath the ramp intended as an imperial carriage entrance, which gives the impression of walking through a grotto before you arrive at the grand staircase built in gaudy polychrome marble. Halfway up, two grandiose caryatids support the entrance to the Amphithéâtre (dress circle), where you can visit a *baignoire* (box) all in red damask and velvet and gaze over the auditorium with its massive chandelier and ceiling painted by Chagall, a controversial addition in 1964. Most opulent of all is the beautifully restored Grand Foyer, laden with marble and sculpted, gilded and painted ceilings that make even Versailles look modest.

The Palais Garnier recently added **L'Opéra**, a space-age red and white restaurant designed by architect Odile Decq, apparently just where Garnier had planned one. If you want to dine in true Garnier surroundings, Garnier also designed the opulent and very expensive **Café de la Paix** (5 place de l'Opéra; tel: 01 40 07 36 36; www.cafedelapaix.fr) across the square.

Palais Garnier; place de l'Opéra; tel: 08 92 89 90 90; www.operadeparis.fr; performances Sept–mid-July, visits daily 10am–5pm, mid-July–Aug until 6pm, 10am–1pm on matinée days; charge; map D5

Explore the network of covered Passages between Palais-Royal and Opéra

Like a cross between Oriental souk and cabinet of curiosities, the 19th-century covered passages were forerunners of the shopping mall or department stores, allowing Parisians to inspect novelties and traverse the town sheltered from the rain and horse-drawn traffic. Several still criss-cross the area between Palais-Royal and Opéra.

Galerie Vivienne (4 rue des Petits-Champs/6 rue Vivienne; map F3), inaugurated in 1826, is defi-

nitely the smartest of the passages (an aspiration revealed in the tag 'Galerie' rather than 'Passage'), with anchors and cornucopias carved on the wooden facades, fanlights and elaborate mosaic floors. Wine merchant **Legrand Filles et Fils** (tel: 01 42 60 07 12), with a huge choice of wines and a tasting counter on the spot, and popular **Bistrot Vivienne** (tel: 01 49 27 00 50) frame the entrance on rue des Petits-Champs; then come shawls and silks at **Wolff et Descourtis**, upmarket *dépôt-vente* (consignment store) **La Marelle**, colourful dresses at **Nathalie Garçon**, and the ladylike tea room **A Priori Thé** (tel: 01 42 97 48 75).

Along the street, **Passage Choiseul** (40 rue des Petits-Champs/23 rue St-Augustin) is shabbier, with cheap snack stalls, dry cleaners and shoe shops – an interloper in this smart banking territory, although garlands of lights give it a jaunty air. This is where writer Céline, whose mother was a lacemaker, grew up in the 1890s, depicted as the gloomy Passage des Bérésinas in *Mort à Credit*.

Passage des Panoramas (11 boulevard Montmartre/10 rue St-Marc) is the earliest of the covered passages. Today it's been colonised

Drouot the auctioneers

Housed in a spiky modern building, **Drouot**, Paris's historic auction house, is a unique institution belonging to 111 *commissaires-priseurs* – specialist auctioneer-valuers – who hold thousands of sales here a year. Unlike the rather stuffy ambience of Sotheby's and Christie's, whose Paris branches are located in the *beaux quartiers* near avenue Matignon, the atmosphere at Drouot is wonderfully frantic. Dealers crowd around the catalogue counter before going up the escalators to the 18 salesrooms, where sales generally take place in the afternoon and viewings are held in the morning and the day before. Goods are fantastically eclectic, with quality and prices varying widely. This is the sort of place you come to with the full intention to view period furniture, 19th-century paintings, early photography or modern art... and find yourself looking in on an auction of Oriental antiquities, jewellery and watches, or fine wines.

Drouot, 9 rue Drouot; tel: 01 48 00 20 20; www.drouot.com; Mon–Sat 11am–6pm, closed mid-Jul–mid-Sept; map F5

by wine bars, bistros, North African and Indian restaurants, including hip wine bar **Coinstot Vino**, gourmet **Passage 53**, and old-fashioned **Bar des Variétés**, with old Paris Match covers glued over the bar.

Directly across the boulevard, **Passage Jouffroy** (10–12 boulevard Montmartre/9 rue de la Grange-Batalière) still most resembles a cabinet of curiosities, with **Grévin** (tel: 01 47 70 85 05; www.grevin-paris.com), the Paris waxworks, on one side, **Café Zéphyr** – one of the few to still have a billiards table – on the other, and the entrance to old-fashioned budget **Hôtel Chopin** (tel: 01 47 70 58 10; www.hotel-chopin.

com) halfway down. Eclectic treasures include walking sticks and curios at **M G Segas**, traditional toys and dolls' house furniture at both **Pain d'Epice** and **La Boîte à Joujoux**, comic books and gems.

Across rue de la Grange-Batalière, **Passage Verdeau** (56 rue de la Grange-Batalière/31bis rue du Fbg-Montmartre) is almost entirely given over to antiques and antiquarian bookshops, and print and picture dealers, in an overflow from the Quartier Drouot (see box). Italian treats are to be had at deli **I Golosi**.

Most passages Mon–Sat, around 8am–8pm; map E4–F5

Go behind the screen at the Grand Rex, an Art Deco cinema with an unusual tour

Inaugurated in front of 3,300 guests in 1932, **Le Grand Rex** is a temple to cinema and a masterpiece of Art Deco style, with its illuminated crown standing out like a beacon against the Paris skyline. French architect Auguste Bluysen and American John Eberson created a fantastical interior perfect for celluloid fantasies, mixing Spanish hacienda, palm trees, Mauresque minarets and classical pediments under a starry ceiling. You can still see films here today, along with rock concerts and special events; but to truly appreciate the building – and the art of cinema – take the clever, and very entertaining, 50-minute interactive **Les Etoiles du Rex** tour. The tour leads you into the projection room and literally behind the screen, letting you into the secrets of sound dubbing, storms and other tricks of the trade and with the chance to ham it up in *King Kong*. And in keeping with the best cinema tradition – there's a neat twist at the end.

The Grands Boulevards are also where you'll find the heart of popular theatreland – or what the French call *théâtre de boulevard*, commercial theatre as opposed to public subsidised venues. Much of it resides in fanciful buildings such as the Théâtre de la Porte St-Martin, Théâtre du Gymnase, Théâtre des Variétés, Théatre des Nouveautés, and Théâtre de la Renaissance, where many plays and operas, for instance Offenbach's *La Belle Hélène*, were premiered in the 19th century.

A recent success is the **Comedy Club**, opened by comedian/actor/entrepreneur Jamel Debbouze, for talent-spotting a multicultural line-up of up-and-coming comedians.

Le Grand Rex; 1 boulevard Poissonnière; www.legrandrex.com; Les Etoiles du Rex tour, school holidays daily 10am–6pm, rest of year Wed–Sun, available in French or English; charge; map G4
Comedy Club; 42 boulevard Bonne Nouvelle; tel: 01 73 54 17 00; www.le comedyclub.fr; charge; map H4

Worship food and classicism at the Madeleine: luxury delis and a showbiz church

The **Eglise de la Madeleine** is about as close as you get to a Roman temple in Paris, a scaled-up version of the Maison Carrée in Nîmes with its colonnaded exterior atop a flight of steps. The foundation stone was laid in 1763 by Louis XV who wanted a showpiece basilica to fill the view from place de la Concorde. After failing to become either a library, bank or opera house during the Revolution, Napoleon plumped for a brash temple to the glory of his Grand Army. With the restoration of the monarchy, the plans reverted to those for a church but Pierre Vignon's temple design was kept. In 1842, the Eglise de la Madeleine was finally consecrated, 80 years after it was begun. The massive bronze doors are modelled on the baptistry doors in Florence, with reliefs depicting the Ten Commandments. Inside is a feast of florid pink, beige and blue marble, gilded friezes, coffered domes and pedimented side altars whose sculptures look far more like Roman generals than religious saints. Napoleon gets a look in too, holding centre stage in a vast mural of the history of Christianity in the half-dome behind the altar.

In the square outside, you can't help feeling, however, that the true French religion holds sway. Prome-

nade around to worship picturesque gâteaux and *traiteur* (caterer) treats at **Fauchon** (No. 24–26; tel: 01 70 39 38 00), with its pink and black shopfronts and gold-plated bakery; fruit sculptures, jams and spices at **Hédiard** (No. 21; tel: 01 43 12 88 88); truffle-flavoured everythings at the **Maison de la Truffe** (No. 19; tel: 01 42 65 53 22), mustard at **Maille** (No. 6; tel: 01 40 15 06 00) and caviar at **Caviar Kaspia** (No. 17; tel: 01 42 65 33 32) and **Prunier** (No. 15; tel: 01 47 42 98 98).

Experience mealtimes in an old workers' canteen at legendary bouillon Chartier

Be prepared to queue and to share tables. A meal at **Chartier** is an experience: a rare surviving example of a *bouillon*, originally a sort of workers' canteen serving soup and stews to hungry workers. Chartier has kept its historic 1890s dining hall with high ceiling, tall mirrors, globe lights and varnished wooden booths, where you might find yourself sharing a table with nostalgics, impoverished Parisians or out-of-towners in search of a bargain. The waiters in long white aprons are a whirlwind of speed, with an incredible capacity for memorising orders and manipulating vast stacks of plates. The food is simple, sustaining and unbelievably cheap, from starters as basic as grated carrot for just €1.90, via decent main courses to a splurge on Mont Blanc (chestnut puree and whipped cream). You're not expected to linger, but before you leave, spot the numbered boxes once allocated to regulars to store their napkins.

Beautiful bouillons

Two other former members of the Chartier chain survive, both with lovely listed art nouveau interiors: **Bouillon Racine** (3 rue Racine, 6th; tel: 01 44 32 15 60; www.bouillon-racine.com), and **Le Montparnasse 1900** (59 boulevard du Montparnasse, 6th; tel: 01 45 49 19 00; www.montparnasse-1900.com), now serving more upmarket, classic brasserie food. Remaining more in the *bouillon* spirit is the vast three-storey **Café du Commerce** (51 rue du Commerce, 15th; tel: 01 45 75 03 27; www.lecafeducommerce.com), opened in 1921 to feed Citroën car workers.

Chartier; 7 rue du Faubourg-Montmartre; tel: 01 47 70 86 29; www.bouillon-chartier. com; daily L and D; map F5
Place de la Madeleine; map B4

Shop 'til you drop at the grands magasins, Galeries Lafayette and Printemps

On boulevard Haussmann, Galeries Lafayette, one of the largest department stores in Europe, and neighbouring rival Printemps, famed for its colossal beauty floor, have been battling it out for over a century. Opened in 1893, **Galeries Lafayette** likes to think it has everything and while it eternally modernises, here and there it still has the feel of an enormous bazaar, a wedding cake of commerce under the huge iron and stained glass dome. Fashion labels run from high-street fashion to luxury tags, the basement claims to be the largest shoe shop in the world and there are over 20 places to eat should you decide you want to spend your life here. Some things could only exist in France, such as the Bordeauxthèque, a temple to Bordeaux wines encompassing an inner circle of mythic vintage grands crus.

Behind its famous corner rotundas, its name picked out in floral mosaics, neighbouring **Printemps**, founded in 1865, has always seen itself as a leader in modernity – the first store to install electricity and fixed prices. Recently it has zapped bling into its gleaming white marble world of luxury, with a ground floor of mini boutiques for luxury shoes and accessories and a first floor of upper-crust jewellery and watches.

In summer, both stores open 'secret' rooftop restaurants with astonishing views.

Galeries Lafayette; 40 boulevard Haussmann; tel: 01 42 82 34 56; www.galerieslafayette.com; Mon–Sat 9.30am–8pm, Thur until 9pm; map D5 Printemps; 64 boulevard Haussmann; tel: 01 42 82 50 00; www.printemps.com; Mon–Sat 9.30am–8pm, Thur until 8.45pm; map C5

CHAMPS-ELYSÉES AND MONCEAU

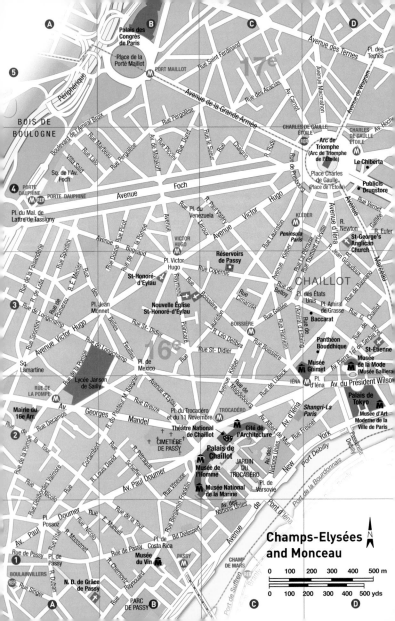

Champs-Elysées and Monceau

Ⓐ Ⓑ Ⓒ Ⓓ

Palais des Congrès de Paris

Place de la Porte Maillot

PORT MAILLOT

Ⓜ PORT MAILLOT

Pl. des Ternes

Avenue des Ternes

Rue Saint Ferdinand

Rue des Acacias

Av. Carnot

17ᵉ

Avenue de la Grande Armée

Av. Mac-Mahon

Avenue de Wagram

Rue Pergolèse

CHARLES DE GAULLE ÉTOILE

Ⓡ CHARLES DE GAULLE ÉTOILE

BOIS DE BOULOGNE

Boulevard de l'Amiral Bruix

Rue Marbeau

Villa Saïd

Rue Pergolèse

Av. de Malakoff

Rue Picot

Rue Duret

Rue Saint-Didier

Rue Rude

Rue de Presbourg

Arc de Triomphe (Arc de Triomphe de l'Étoile)

Le Chiberta

Place Charles de Gaulle (Place de l'Étoile)

Publicis Drugstore

Sq. de l'Av. Foch

Ⓐ PORTE DAUPHINE

PORTE DAUPHINE

Pl. du Mal. de Lattre de Tassigny

Avenue Foch

Rue Vernet

Rue Euler

R. Newton

St-George's Anglican Church

R. Jean Giraudoux

Avenue d'Iéna

KLÉBER

Ⓜ KLÉBER

Peninsula Paris

Rue Lauriston

Avenue Victor Hugo

Pl. du Venezuela

Rue Leroux

Avenue Kléber

Rue de Belloy

CHAILLOT

Rue Dumont d'Urville

R. de Bassano

Rue de Longchamp

R.E. Mathet

Rue des

Rue de la Pompe

Rue Boissière

Rue Copernic

Réservoirs de Passy

VICTOR HUGO

Ⓜ VICTOR HUGO

Pl. Victor Hugo

St-Honoré-d'Eylau

Pl. des États Unis

Pl. Amiral de Grasse

Baccarat

Ⓐ Rue de Longchamp

Rue Desbordes

Pl. Jean Monnet

Rue Dosne

Rue Bugeaud

Belles

Feuilles

Rue St-Didier

Nouvelle Église St-Honoré-d'Eylau

R. Léo Delibes

BOISSIÈRE

Ⓜ BOISSIÈRE

Rue Galilée

Rue d'Iéna

Rue de Lübeck

Panthéon Bouddhique

St-Étienne

Musée de la Mode (Musée Galliera)

16ᵉ

Rue Poincaré

Rue St-Didier

Rue Hamelin

Musée Guimet

Ⓜ IÉNA

Av. Pierre 1er de Serbie

Sq. Lamartine

Pl. de Mexico

Avenue d'Eylau

Rue Boissière

Pl. d'Iéna

Av. du Président Wilson

Palais de Tokyo

Ⓜ

Lycée Janson de Sailly

Rue du Dr. Blanche

Rue Greuze

Pl. du Trocadéro et du 11 Novembre

TROCADÉRO

Ⓜ TROCADÉRO

Avenue Albert de Mun

Musée d'Art Moderne de la Ville de Paris

RUE DE LA POMPE

Ⓜ

Mairie du 16e Arr.

Av. Georges Mandel

Rue du Pasteur M. Boegner

Théâtre National de Chaillot

Cité de l'Architecture

Shangri-La Paris

Rue Decamps

CIMETIÈRE DE PASSY

Palais de Chaillot

Ⓜ

JARDIN DU TROCADÉRO

Rue Fresnel

Rue de la Pompe

R. Cortambert

R. Petraque

R. Schaeffer

R. Louis David

Av. Paul Doumer

Rue Vineuse

Musée de l'Homme

Musée National de la Marine

Av. du Président Wilson

Av. de New York

Port Debilly

Passerelle Debilly

Rue Benjamin Franklin

Rue de la Tour

Rue Desbordes Valmore

Pl. Possoz

Rue Nicolo

Pl. Doumer

Rue E. Manuel

Pl. de Costa Rica

Av. des Nations Unies

Av. de Varsovie

Port d'Iéna

Pont d'Iéna

Av. Paul Doumer

Rue Scheffer

Rue Raynouard

Rue de Passy

Musée du Vin

Ⓜ

PASSY

Ⓜ PASSY

CHAMP DE MARS

Port de la Bourdonnais

Ⓐ Av. Paul Doumer

Rue du Ranelagh

Pl. de Passy

RUE DE PASSY

BOULAINVILLIERS

Ⓡ

Rue Singer

N. D. de Grâce de Passy

Rue Duban

R. Chernoviz

R. Raynouard

Ⓑ PARC DE PASSY

Pont de Bir-Hakeim

Av. de Suffren

Quai Branly

N

Champs-Elysées and Monceau

| 0 | 100 | 200 | 300 | 400 | 500 m |

| 0 | 100 | 200 | 300 | 400 | 500 yds |

Ⓐ Ⓑ Ⓒ Ⓓ

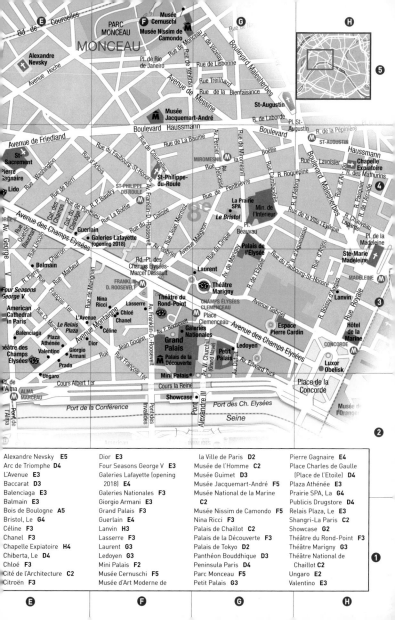

Get into the spirit of 1900 at the Grand Palais, Petit Palais and Pont Alexandre III

The grand triumvirate put up for the Exposition Universelle of 1900 still captures the glitter of the Belle Epoque and the optimism of the new century, showcasing all that was new in arts, technology and industry.

A bravura exercise in steel, glass and stone, with the largest glass roof in Europe, crowned by two bronze ensembles of galloping horses, the **Grand Palais** (www. grandpalais.fr; map F3) exudes Belle Epoque confidence in its sheer size, wealth of decoration and unselfconsciously eclectic mix of styles – Classical motifs here, Art Nouveau flourishes there – perhaps not surprising as, after 260 architects entered the competition in 1896, its three facades were actually designed by three different architects, Henri Deglane, Albert Louvet and Albert Thomas. Around 50 million visitors flocked to the fair in 1900. Later, the grand **Nave** (avenue Winston Churchill) was used for artistic salons, motor shows and domestic appliance fairs. During World War II, it housed Nazi tanks; in 1994 it closed overnight when a metal beam fell off the roof, reopening only in 2005. It now houses all manner of events and salons, from the giant art installations of Monumenta (Kiefer, Serra, Boltan-

ski and Kapoor, so far), to exclusive fashion shows and showjumping. The avenue Eisenhower wing contains the **Galeries Nationales** (tel: 01 44 13 17 17) used for prestigious, crowd-pulling art exhibitions, and the avenue Franklin-Roosevelt wing contains the old-fashioned **Palais de la Découverte** (tel: 01 56 43 20 20; www.palais-decouverte.fr) science museum.

Crown your visit with a meal, or the luxury snacks served all afternoon, at **Mini Palais** (tel: 01 42 56 42 42; www.minipalais.com), the Grand Palais's glamorous restaurant decorated to resemble a 19th-century artist's studio.

Although the Grand Palais grabs

most of the attention, the **Petit Palais** (tel: 01 53 43 40 00; www.petit palais.paris.fr; map G3) across the street is another fanciful confection of coloured marble, mosaics and wrought iron. Today, many people come here for the temporary exhibitions, but the eclectic fine art collection of the Ville de Paris offers plenty of discoveries: works by Bonnard and Cézanne and a gallery of showstopper art nouveau vases made for the Great Exhibition.

The most surprising part of the ensemble? Probably, **Pont Alexandre III** built as a link to Les Invalides across the Seine – with a cacophony of ships and dolphins, trident-bearing cherubs and fancy lampposts

1900 fever

A few other buildings survive from the enthusiasm for all things 1900: Le Train Bleu, the opulent brasserie inside Gare de Lyon, beautiful Art Nouveau Brasserie Julien and, of course, Gare d'Orsay, no longer a train station.

with lion's paws – whose name, at the time, some disliked for its association with imperial Russia. You can even go inside the bridge, where venue the **Showcase** (under Pont Alexandre III, Port des Champs-Elysées; tel: 01 45 61 25 43; www. showcase.fr; map G2) hosts bands and DJs at weekends in secret rooms with watery views.

Window shop on avenue Montaigne and Faubourg-St-Honoré

The mere mention of avenue Montaigne evokes the mythic world of haute-couture. The luxurious *Triangle d'Or* (golden triangle) formed by avenues Montaigne, George-V and rue François-1er is a world away from the nearby Champs-Elysées. Couture and upmarket ready-to-wear labels provide impressive window-shopping, the impression of exclusivity often reinforced by the setting – aristocratic houses set back behind iron railings.

On avenue Montaigne, you'll find the distinctive pearl-grey facade of **Dior** (No. 30), where Christian Dior revolutionised fashion with the New Look in 1957, along with classic houses **Ungaro** (No. 2), **Nina Ricci** (No. 39), **Valentino** (No. 17), **Chanel** (No. 42), **Chloé** (No. 44) and

Céline (No. 36), and Italians **Prada** (No. 10) and **Giorgio Armani** (No. 18). Nearby, there's **Balenciaga** (10 avenue George-V), back at the top with superb cuts and beautiful leatherware designed by Demna Gvasalia, and **Balmain** (44 rue François-1er). At lunchtime, the sunglasses set hangs out at **L'Avenue** (No. 41; tel: 01 40 70 14 91; www.avenue-restaurant.com), the fashionable Costes brasserie, while at night, they survey the city from **La Maison Blanche** (No. 15; tel: 01 47 23 55 99; www.maison-blanche.fr), the modern eatery perched atop the Théâtre des Champs-Elysées.

There's a second designer fashion nucleus on the other side of the Champs-Elysées along **rue du Faubourg-St-Honoré**, where upmarket French and Italian labels follow in the footsteps of **Lanvin** at No. 22. Here Jeanne Lanvin set up as a *modiste* in 1889, later one of the first designers to introduce sportswear and perfume lines in the 1920s. No. 22 is now the womenswear shop, while the menswear boutique at No. 15 still has some of its 1920s Art Deco furniture by Armand-Albert Rateau.

Triangle d'Or; map E3
Rue du Faubourg-St Honoré; map G-H3

Dine with the powerbrokers at ministerial favourites Laurent and Lasserre

Conveniently close to the Elysée Palace and the Ministry of the Interior, salmon-coloured **Laurent** (41 avenue Gabriel; tel: 01 42 25 00 39; www.le-laurent.com; map F3) is particularly splendid in summer when dining is under parasols bordering the Champs-Elysées gardens, yet discretely shielded from the hoi polloi. The food is wonderful (modern French made with seasonal produce), and the outdoor setting makes it one of the most relaxed of Paris's top restaurants.

Similarly, although international foodies flock to Alain Ducasse at the Plaza Athénée, when it comes to a business lunch you're more likely to catch politicians, and media and business magnates discussing strategy in **Le Relais Plaza** (21 avenue Montaigne; tel: 01 53 67 64 00; www.plaza-athenee-paris. com; map E3), its adjoining, slightly more casual, Art Deco brasserie.

Lasserre (17 avenue Franklin-Roosevelt; tel: 01 43 59 02 13; www.restaurant-lasserre.com; map F3) is a legend for its *pigeon Malraux* (pigeon stuffed with foie gras), created for then-minister of culture André Malraux who lunched here every day in the 1960s, and the retractable roof. An almost unbelievable number of staff hover with trays and bottles, but the restaurant has recently had an injection of energy with the arrival of young chef Adrien Trouilloud.

At sleek modern **Le Chiberta** (3 rue Arsène-Houssaye; tel: 01 53 53 42 00; www.lechiberta.com; map D4), you can dine amid modern art or at the bar. Run by Guy Savoy, star turns from his gastronomic restaurant include grapefruit terrine with Earl Grey sauce.

If you do one three star, perhaps make it **Pierre Gagnaire** (6 rue Balzac; tel: 01 58 36 12 50; www. pierre-gagnaire.com; map E4), where the relatively affordable business lunch menu gives an insight into Gagnaire's light, fabulously inventive cuisine.

Have tea with Tiepolo at the Musée Jacquemart-André

A Tiepolo in the tea room is just a hint of the grand lifestyle and superb artworks amassed by a couple of fervent art collectors.

Edouard André, scion of a rich banking family, and his artist wife Nélie Jacquemart built this grand mansion in 1869–75 to house the collection they had picked up on their travels or unearthed in auction houses. It gives a vision of grand 19th-century living, with its galleried music room – where the couple hosted concerts and balls – Moorish-style smoking room, hung with English portraits, winter garden with pot plants, and the extravagant double staircase,

decorated with a grand fresco by Tiepolo, originally painted for the Villa Contarini. Upstairs, Nelie's former studio became their 'Italian museum' whose treasures include a small Botticelli, Uccello's jewel-like *St George and the Dragon*, and glazed terracotta reliefs by the della Robbia family.

The museum reflects the magpie, eclectic eye of these collectors but also their impeccable taste. Even the 18th-century portraits, now often seen as dull and pompous are of exceptional quality, for instance a charming portrait by Nattier of the *Mathilde de Canisy*, with a garland of flowers and a shimmery satin dress, and Elizabeth Vigée-Lebrun's luminous *Countess Catherine Skavronskaia*. In the library, Dutch paintings include Rembrandt's *The Pilgrims of Emmaus*, the small canvas illuminated by a shaft of light.

As to tea with Tiepolo: the former dining room is now an elegant café and salon de thé, its walls hung with tapestries and Tiepolo resplendent on the ceiling.

Musée Jacquemart-André; 158 boulevard Haussmann; tel: 01 45 62 11 59; www.musee-jacquemart-andre.com; daily 10am–6pm; charge; map F5

Go on a mini tour of France at the Cité de l'Architecture

Medieval monuments and modern architecture give an intriguing double identity to the **Cité de l'Architecture**. The sweeping ground-floor gallery is like a mini tour of France via the doorways and past sculpted pinnacles of a hit list of Romanesque and Gothic churches. Full-size reproductions of the Last Judgement from the church at Conques, the medieval tomb of the Dukes of Burgundy and 300 others add up to a tour de force of plaster casting. On the first floor, there's a dim succession of mysterious frescoed church interiors before the second floor leaps into the mid 19th century and modernity, with iron structures and skyscrapers, architectural maquettes, film archives, Paris's circular Maison de la Radio and a spectacular full-size mock-up of one of the duplex apartments in Le Corbusier's Cité Radieuse, in Marseille. The Cité also puts on temporary exhibitions in huge basement galleries. The museum's setting, the Palais de Chaillot, is itself a monument of imposing Modernist classical revival architecture put up for the world fair of 1937 and also home to the Musée de la Marine (Maritime Museum; tel: 01 53 65 69 53; www. musee-marine.fr/paris; closing

down for renovation 2017–20) the Musée de l'Homme (tel: 01 44 05 72 72; www.museedelhomme.fr) – the recently renovated state-of-the-art anthropology museum where Picasso used to go to look at African masks – and the Théâtre National de Chaillot (theatre and dance; tel: 01 53 65 30 00; www.theatre-chaillot.fr).

Cité de l'Architecture; Palais de Chaillot, 1 place du Trocadéro; tel: 01 58 51 52 00; www.citechaillot.fr; Mon, Wed, Fri–Sun 11am–7pm, Thur 11am–9pm; charge; map C2

See a late night art show at the Palais de Tokyo

If you're in the mood for adventurous art, check out what's on at contemporary art space the **Palais de Tokyo**. The art is international, experimental and often highly conceptual and you may feel you need a dose of theory to understand it; but the Palais does its best to make its shows accessible – gallery attendants are all trained mediators. Occupying a vast modernist classical pavilion built for the 1937 Exposition Internationale, the interior looks deliberately unfinished, which gives it a slightly underground appeal, especially at night when it's open until mid-

night. There's an art bookshop in a cage, trendy restaurant Tokyo Eat and the very cool BlackBlock gift shop, where eclectic items from inexpensive badges to artists' limited editions are shown in fridge cabinets. Outside, 16 amateur gardeners have created their own little corners of paradise.

During the day, the Palais de Tokyo can be combined with the **Musée d'Art Moderne de la Ville de Paris**, the municipal museum of modern art, which occupies the other wing. The permanent collection is strong on Cubism, Orphism, the Ecole de Paris, and works by Arp and Fautrier. Be sure to look at Raoul Dufy's vast mural *La Fée Electricité* (The Electricity Fairy). Painted for the 1937 electricity pavilion, it is a joyous celebration of electrical power and all those behind it, from Greek gods to Watt and Ampère.

Palais de Tokyo; 13 avenue du Président-Wilson; tel: 01 47 23 54 01; www.palais detokyo.com; Wed–Mon noon–midnight; charge; map D2
Musée d'Art Moderne de la Ville de Paris; 11 avenue du Président-Wilson; tel: 01 53 67 40 00; www.mam.paris.fr; Tue–Sun 10am–6pm; collection free, charge for temporary exhibitions; map D2

Find reasons to celebrate on the Champs-Elysées, laid out as Napoleon's triumphal way

Much of the time it's hard to understand the fuss about the Champs-Elysées, automatically dubbed 'the most beautiful avenue in the world' by the French – but the Champs do come into their own for national celebrations, such as the military parade on *le Quatorze Juillet* (Bastille Day) and the finale of the Tour de France.

The Champs were first laid out as a promenade by royal gardener André Le Nôtre in an extension of the Tuileries gardens, later forming Napoleon's triumphal way to the Arc de Triomphe. The lower half near place de la Concorde still has a pleasure garden feel, with the pavilions of restaurants Ledoyen (map G3) and Laurent (see page 71), and theatres Marigny and Rond-Point.

In the late 19th century, it became a fashionable residential street. A few traces of grandeur remain in the mansions of the Rond-Point des Champs-Elysées, the Hôtel de la Païva (No. 25), the original Guerlain perfume store (No. 68), Le Fouquet's brasserie (No. 97) and Louis Vuitton's glitzy flagship store at No. 101. At the top is the celebrated **Publicis Drugstore** (No. 133; www.publicisdrugstore.com) founded by advertising maestro Marcel Bleustein-Blanchet in the 1950s.

It contains an upmarket deli, cigar shop, international newsagent, cinemas and the Atelier Etoile de Joël Robuchon (tel: 01 47 23 75 75; www.joel-robuchon.com). The new flagship store of Galeries Lafayette, designed by Danish architect Bjarke Ingels, is due to open at No.52 in 2018. At the western end, the **Arc de Triomphe** is another of Napoleon's showstoppers, modelled on the Arch of Titus in Rome but bigger, inaugurated in 1836 long after his downfall. A climb to the top rewards you with entrancing views of the traffic milling around below.

Arc de Triomphe; place de l'Etoile (access by underpass); tel: 01 55 37 73 77; www.arc-de-triomphe.monuments-nationaux.fr; daily 10am–11pm, winter until 10.30pm; charge; map D4

Mix with the privileged beau monde at Parc Monceau

Parc Monceau was created in the 1770s by Philippe Egalité, Duc d'Orléans, brother of Louis XVI, who filled it with picturesque follies – a pyramid, an antique colonnade around the lake, a Venetian bridge over the stream – amid rolling lawns and magnificent trees. Ever-popular with the area's nannies and well-bred schoolchildren, the park is at the heart of a privileged residential district built up since the mid-19th century. Some put up mini French châteaux here (such as the Musée Jacquemart-André, see page 72), others had more exotic tastes – witness the red lacquered chinoiserie house at 48 rue de Courcelles, built for an Oriental art dealer. Russian émigrés constructed **Alexandre Nevsky Russian Orthodox Cathedral** (12 rue Daru; tel: 01 42 27 37 24), with five towers topped by onion domes.

Overlooking the park, two of the fine mansions are now museums. The **Musée Nissim de Camondo** was erected in 1911 by Moïse de Camondo, a wealthy banker from Constantinople, in a style quite out of its time yet with all mod cons, who filled it with a fabulous collection of 18th-century decorative arts: Sèvres and Meissen porcelain, Aubusson carpets and Beauvais tapestries.

Another grand mansion belonged to banker and voyager Henri Cernuschi, a refugee Italian revolutionary who made a fortune in banking before touring Asia in 1871–2. A giant Japanese buddha and the Chinese pots he brought back formed the foundations of the **Musée Cernuschi**, which is particularly strong on Chinese ceramics and funerary figures.

Musée Cernuschi; 7 avenue Vélasquez; tel: 01 53 96 21 50; www.cernuschi.paris.fr; Tue–Sun 10am–6pm; free; map F5
Musée Nissim de Camondo; 63 de Monceau; tel: 01 53 89 06 50; www.lesarts decoratifs.fr; Wed–Sun 10am–5.30pm; charge; map F5
Parc Monceau; 55 boulevard de Courcelles (other entrances on avenues Vélasquez, Van Dyck, Ruysdael); www.paris.fr; daily summer 7am–9/10pm, winter 7am–8pm; free; map F5

Atone for Louis XVI and Marie-Antoinette at the Chapelle Expiatoire

In a slightly forgotten corner between the Madeleine and boulevard Haussmann, the **Chapelle Expiatoire** is a small masterpiece of neoclassical architecture and one of the most moving reminders of the French Revolution. Located on the site of the former cemetery of the Madeleine, where the guillotined bodies of Louis XVI and Marie-Antoinette were thrown into a pit in 1793, the golden stone chapel was commissioned by restoration monarch Louis XVIII (brother of Louis XVI) and built 1816–26 by Fontaine, one of the architects of the rue de Rivoli for Napoleon.

A beautifully pared-back entrance pavilion hides the chapel itself, which is reached at the rear of a courtyard past stylised tombs in memory of the Swiss guards massacred when protecting the king and queen at the Tuileries palace in 1792. Inside the chapel, face to face, stand two white marble statues: Marie-Antoinette accompanied by Religion bearing a cross (by Cortot), and Louis XVI ascending to heaven with an angel (by Bosio).

The chapel long had a dubious reputation as a gathering point for reactionary royalists, and was even nearly demolished in the 1880s to make way for a station. But here, more so than at any other of the city's revolutionary sights, the calm and sobriety of the architecture combine to create something incredibly mournful and elegiac.

Chapelle Expiatoire; Square Louis XVI, 29 rue Pasquier; tel: 01 42 65 35 80; www.chapelle-expiatoire.monuments-nationaux.fr; Apr–Oct Thur–Sat 10am–5.30pm; charge; map H4

Find your inner zen and a serene Japanese garden at the Musée Guimet and Panthéon Bouddhique

A seven-headed snake from Cambodia's Angkor Wat temple complex now provides a lead to the collection of beautifully poised Khmer sculptures which form the centrepiece of the **Musée Guimet** (pictured), the national collection of Asian art. Here you really are in another, zen, world peopled by Hindu and Buddhist gods each more rounded and beatifically smiling than the last. Other highlights include Tibetan tantras and sculptures from Afghanistan.

While the main museum is beautifully displayed, with sober, uncluttered calm, the **Panthéon Bouddhique**, a few doors up the street, gives a better idea of Emile Guimet's original vision of a museum dedicated to religions and popular worship. Here, the ranks of bronze and painted wood gods, deities and sacred temple figures amassed on a journey to Japan in 1876 give the feel of an Oriental shrine, a journey extended by the bamboo and stepping stones in the small Japanese garden and the tea pavilion at the rear.

For a very chic place to eat, continue up to place des Etats-Unis. Here, glass manufacturer **Baccarat** has its splendid Parisian showrooms, museum gallery and the Cristal Room (tel: 01 40 22 11 10; www.cristalroom.com) restaurant in rooms given a brilliantly tongue-in-cheek decor by Philippe Starck – with food overseen by Grand Véfour chef Guy Martin and magnificent chandeliers, naturally.

Musée (National des Arts Asiatiques) Guimet; 6 place d'Iéna; tel: 01 56 52 53 00; www.guimet.fr; Wed–Mon 10am–6pm; charge; map D3
Panthéon Bouddhique; 19 avenue d'Iéna; tel: 01 40 73 88 00; www.guimet.fr; Wed–Mon 9.45am–5.45pm; free; map D3
Baccarat; 11 place des Etats-Unis; tel: 01 01 40 22 11 10; www.baccarat.fr; museum gallery Mon, Wed–Sat 10am–6pm; charge; map D3

Enjoy being pampered like a queen at the luxury George V spa

Resembling a scene from Marie-Antoinette's Versailles (the Sofia Coppola version), The Spa at the **Four Seasons George V** (pictured) is a sexy, soft-focus take on period grandeur, where Louis XVI chairs, misty landscapes and *toile de jouy* prints are the backdrop for all manner of treatments – with the bonus of a great pool. Its ultimate treat has to be 'A stroll through Versailles', a 2.5 hr skin-softening, energy-boosting package inspired by the 18th-century queen, where you are pampered with an orange blossom body scrub followed by a shea butter massage, ending with a milky facial and some *macarons*.

Today's luxury hotels rival each other with ever more luxurious spas and both exotic and exclusive solutions to stress, jetlag and advancing age. At the **Shangri-La** near the Palais de Chaillot, chic French Carita brand products are on the spa menu along with body treatments by KOS and eastern-inspired 'ceremonies' from Thémaé, including a green-tea facial. The Relaxing Day Package (€400) comprises a facial, a body treatment and access to the Health Club, whose terrace overlooks the Eiffel Tower.

The La Prairie Spa at **Le Bristol** is a soothing candlelit environment for a programme of age-fighting, anti-stress treatments using the Swiss luxury brand's hi-tech cellular products. In a 19th-century Haussmannian building, the Peninsula Spa at the five-star **Peninsula Paris** has a good choice of aromatherapy, ayurvedic and organic treatments. The sleek pool, with a floor-to-ceiling waterfall, is one of the best hotel pools in town.

Four Seasons George V; 31 avenue George V; tel: 01 49 52 72 10; www.fourseasons. com/paris; map E3
Shangri-La; 10 avenue d'Iéna; tel: 01 53 67 19 78; www.shangri-la.com/paris; map C2
Le Bristol; 108 rue du Faubourg-St-Honoré; tel: 01 42 66 24 22; www.lebristol paris.com; map G4
Peninsula Paris; 19 avenue Kléber; tel: 01 58 12 66 82; www. peninsula.com/paris; map page 48 C4

MONTMARTRE AND PIGALLE

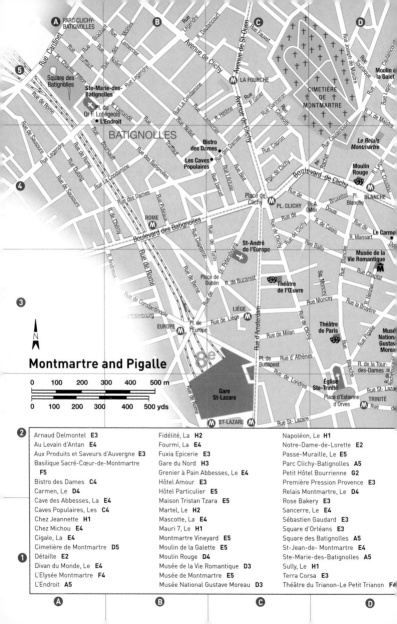

Montmartre and Pigalle

0 100 200 300 400 500 m

0 100 200 300 400 500 yds

8e

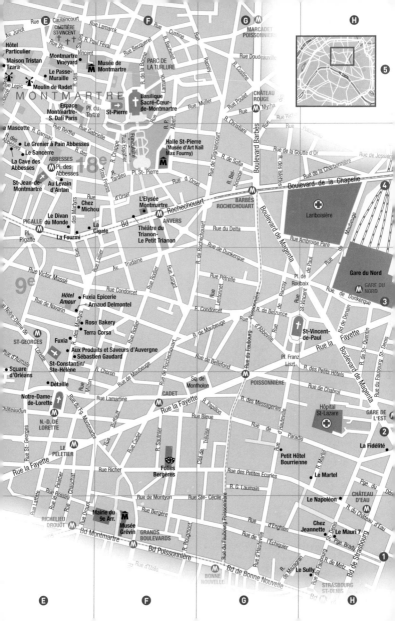

Walk through walls in hilly Montmartre and access quiet streets, pretty cottages and an ancient vineyard

A bronze head, hand and a trousered leg emerge strangely from a wall on place Marcel Aymé, a reference to Marcel Aymé's 1943 short story *Le passe-muraille* about Dutilleul, a civil servant who discovers he can walk through walls. Using his skill to rob jewellers, he finally comes to a literally sticky end – stuck in the wall – pretty much where the sculpture is. Today, this perhaps serves as a good metaphor for exploring the area: once past overcrowded place du Tertre you'll find you can still slip into quiet, deserted streets, with picturesque cottages and artists' studios, and take short cuts by steep stairways.

Place du Tertre is at the junction of rue Norvins, where Aymé lived, and avenue Junot, with its unusual houses, notably the **Maison Tristan Tzara** at No. 15, designed in 1926 by Austrian architect Adolphe Loos; and the **Hôtel Particulier** at No. 23 (tel: 01 53 41 81 40; www.hotel-particulier-montmartre.com), an exclusive five-room hotel entered off a stairway, past an overgrown lump of rock known as the witch's stone.

In the other direction, rue des Saules descends past the **Montmartre vineyard**, a relic of the vines that once covered the district. The grapes are harvested with much pomp every October and carried in a costumed procession to the town hall.

Overlooking the vines, the endearingly old-fashioned **Musée de Montmartre** occupies a manor house where Auguste Renoir rented a studio; a recent renovation programme included replanting the gardens as they were when he painted them.

Musée de Montmartre; 12 rue Cortot; tel: 01 49 25 89 37; www.museedemontmartre. fr; daily 10am–6pm; charge; map E5

Observe local characters in the bars of Abbesses – also officially home to the best baguette in Paris

Part of Montmartre's appeal lies in its many facets. Just seconds from a tourist trap you can be in authentic, lived-in Paris or at a corner café packed with eclectic locals – and in Abbesses, arty types or a drag queen are equally likely.

Place des Abbesses has one of Paris's two métro stations still with its Art Nouveau glass canopy by Hector Guimard, and a small garden where a tiled wall reads 'I love you' in 300 languages. Across the square, take a look inside the curious church of **St-Jean-de-Montmartre**. Behind its brick facade studded with turquoise ceramics, the church built in 1894–1904 was a pioneer in the use of reinforced concrete.

Rue des Abbesses is sprinkled with good food shops, although its one-off clothes shops are slowly being replaced by chains.

Good places for a breather are busy bar **Le Sancerre** (No. 35; tel: 01 42 58 08 20); wine merchants **La Cave des Abbesses** (No. 43; tel: 01 42 52 81 54), with a few tables outside in summer and a tiny wine bar at the rear where you can try different wines, and there's a real fire in winter; and **La Mascotte** (No. 52; tel: 01 46 06 28 15), an old-fashioned brasserie that still draws a

dedicated crowd of offbeat regulars for oysters and steaks.

There's clearly something in the hill air. Two bakers on the street have won the city's prize for the best baguette in Paris: Pascal Barillon at **Au Levain d'Antan** (No. 6) in 2011 and Djibril Bodian at **Le Grenier à Pain** (No. 38) in 2010 and 2015.

Abbesses; map E4

Visit Symbolist artist Gustave Moreau at his home and studio

With hundreds of paintings covering the walls and thousands of drawings and studies that you can pull out on wooden shutters, the double-storey studio of Symbolist artist Gustave Moreau (1826–98) constitutes one of the most captivating and eccentric museums in Paris, testimony to the artist's feverish creativity. Inspired by mythology and the Bible, Renaissance painting, the Orient and India, some of Moreau's pet subjects – such as lascivious Salome, or Oedipus and the Sphinx – appear again and again. There are centaurs, unicorns and other mystical beasts, fantastical architecture, mysterious caves and forests in dreamy works at once charged with detail and alternating with darker, broader patches pierced by intense spots of colour. Amid highly finished paintings you'll find works in progress, along with a case of unusual, red wax sculptures used as working models to plot out compositions. Although you can see Moreau's paintings in museums, here you get a true idea of his ferment of ideas and the artist's own vision of immortality.

During his lifetime, Moreau had planned for his studio to become a museum, transforming the building, which he left with all its contents to the state, and appointing his favourite pupil, the painter Georges Rouault, as first curator. Even the downstairs apartment was part of his schema. Although it looks every bit the image of cluttered 19th-century living, it was arranged symbolically by the artist as a sort of conceptual artwork in its own right.

Musée National Gustave Moreau; 14 rue de la Rochefoucauld; tel: 01 48 74 38 50; www.musee-moreau.fr; Mon, Wed, Thu 10am–12.45pm, 2–5.15pm, Fri–Sun 10am–5.15pm; charge; map D3

Admire the pathos at Montmartre cemetery

Originally gypsum quarries, then a gruesome mass grave for victims of the Revolution before becoming the city's new northern cemetery in 1825, today, the **Cimetière de Montmartre** is romantically overgrown, with rows of tombs and emotive sculptures of weeping nymphs, doom figures, distraught maidens, and an unlikely copy of Michelangelo's *Moses*.

Many of the people buried here are intrinsic to the artistic history of the area, among them society courtesan Alphonsine Plessis (also known as Marie Duplessis). Mistress first of Alexandre Dumas fils (son), later of Liszt and then the Comte of Perregaux, before dying of tuberculosis in 1847 aged just 23, she was the model for Marguerite Gautier in Dumas's *La Dame aux Camélias* and Violetta in Verdi's *La Traviata*.

Other graves include composers Jacques Offenbach and Hector Berlioz, artists Gustave Moreau (see page 86) and Edgar Degas, in a family vault marked Famille de Gas, dancers Nijinsky – sculpted in bronze as Harlequin – and Louise Weber, alias the Moulin Rouge's La Goulue, with an epitaph 'creatrice of the cancan', as well as new wave film director François Truffaut.

The most visited tomb of all is probably that of Dalida, stage name for Yolanda Gigliotti, Italo-Egyptian singer and gay icon, who committed suicide in 1987. Her dramatic tomb (on the terraces to the right of the entrance), portraying the singer in front of a triumphal arch and sunburst, is always strewn with flowers. You can also see the fanciful turreted house where she lived at 23 rue d'Orchampt, and a bronze bust on nearby place Dalida.

Cimetière de Montmartre; 20 avenue Rachel; tel: 01 53 42 36 30; www.paris.fr, Mon–Fri 8am–6pm, Sat 8.30am–6pm, Sun 9am–6pm, closes 5.30pm in winter; free; map D5

Empathise with the Romantics: George Sand, Chopin and Ary Scheffer at the Musée de la Vie Romantique

A lock of hair, plaster casts of her and Frederic Chopin's hands, family portraits, watercolours, her great grandfather's snuffbox and desk create a gentle shrine to George Sand and Romanticism in the pretty green-shuttered house once belonging to Dutch-born artist Ary Scheffer. Nevertheless, the **Musée de la Vie Romantique** comes more in the spirit of romantic melancholia than sublime passion, and as such is surely far too prim for Sand – alias Amantine-Aurore Lucile Dupin, prolific novelist, playwright and journalist, bohemian, cigar smoker and liberated woman, who dared shock society by divorcing her husband and taking a succession of prominent lovers.

Upstairs you'll find portraits and historic paintings by Ary Scheffer, a successful society portrait painter and friend of Napoleon, as well as other decidedly minor 19th-century artists. Scheffer's two high-ceilinged, north-facing studios across the courtyard are now used for exhibitions. A pleasant tea room opens in the garden conservatory during summer.

Scheffer was more inspiring as a host than as a painter, inviting the artists and intellectuals of the day to his salons and soirées. Delacroix (who taught drawing to Sand's son Maurice), Liszt, Rossini, Turgenev and Charles Dickens were all guests here, as well as Sand and Chopin.

Musée de la Vie Romantique; 16 rue Chaptal, 75009; tel: 01 55 31 95 67; www.vie-romantique.paris.fr; Tue–Sun 10am–6pm; free; map D3

Discover La Nouvelle Athènes, including the house where Bizet is said to have penned *Carmen*

The Musée de la Vie Romantique is a good starting point for exploring the district, which was an intellectual hub in the early 19th century, dubbed the Nouvelle Athènes for its colony of writers, artists, composers and actors, as well as *lorettes* – the lavishly dressed demi-mondaines who frequented the area around Notre-Dame-de-Lorette.

So where did George Sand actually live? She divided her time between the family home at Nohant in the Creuse and Paris, living in rue Pigalle before moving, in 1842, to **Square d'Orléans**. An elegant private garden square, designed in 1830 by English architect Edward Crecy, during the week you can nonetheless wander into it from 80 rue Taitbout. Lovers Sand and Chopin rented facing apartments at Nos 5 and 9 where she lived with her two children and Chopin had space to compose.

The area is peppered with fine private residences from the days before the 19th-century uniformisation of Paris by civic planner Georges-Eugène Haussmann – such as on place St-Georges, with its neo-Renaissance *hôtels particuliers*; on rue St-Lazare and rue Notre-Dame-de-Lorette, where Delacroix had a studio; or at 26 rue de la Tour d'Auvergne, where

Georges Bizet was born in 1838. The prettiest of the lot are on **rue de la Tour-des-Dames** – home to the famous actor Talma whose portrait was painted by Delacroix – and actresses Madame Mars, a star at the Comédie Française, who lived in the elegant villa at No. 1, and Mademoiselle Duchesnois, who lived in the unusual semi-circular No. 3. There's more Bizet at 22 rue de Douai/34 rue Duperré, where cocktail bar **Le Carmen** (tel: 01 45 26 50 00; map D4) now occupies the extravagant period salons, complete with mouldings and sculpted caryatids, of the house where Bizet is said to have written *Carmen*.

Square d'Orléans; map E3

Survey the city from the Sacré-Cœur

The sugary white church of **Sacré-Cœur** is one of those buildings you suddenly glimpse in the distance from some of the most unlikely spots in Paris, partly because it stands on a hill, partly because it is built in travertine limestone that secretes calcite when it rains, keeping the stone perpetually white. It was built between 1875 and 1919 as an act of penance for France's defeat in the 1870 Franco-Prussian War and the succeeding Commune, caused, some believed, by a national lack of religion since the French Revolution. The church was paid for by public subscription, with donors' names carved in the stone, and located

on the hill where Saint Denis was martyred in the 3rd century – hence 'martyr's mount' (Montmartre), although the name could also come from an even earlier temple to Mars that is thought to have stood here. Architect Paul Abadie designed the basilica in a Romano-Byzantine style with a clutter of domes and bronze equestrian statues of Joan of Arc and St Louis, two symbols of the French nation, over the portico. Inside it's gloriously kitsch, with a vast glittery mosaic in the apse, more mosaics in the side chapels and a huge vaulted crypt with statues of saints. If you've got the energy, you can climb up to the top of the dome, although the views are also pretty good from the parvis outside the church, with its tiers of steps, or from the gardens of square Wilmotte that meander round to the side. In keeping with Montmartre's belief that it is a mountain and not simply a hill, you can also reach the church by funicular (fare: one metro ticket).

Basilica Sacré-Cœur-de-Montmartre; place du Parvis du Sacré-Cœur; www.sacre-coeur-montmartre.com; daily 6am–10.30pm, dome summer 8.30am–8pm, winter 9am–5pm, crypt times vary; charge for dome; map F5

Catch a concert, an accordion fest or a cheeky drag show in the old music halls of Pigalle

Montmartre's past as a place for weekend entertainment lives on in a string of fanciful concert halls amid the peep shows and souvenir stalls of boulevard Rochechouart. **L'Elysée Montmartre** (No. 72; www.elysee-montmartre.com), opened in 1807, is said to have seen the birth of the cancan. Now one of Paris's best spots for rock, roots and the long-running Sunday *Bal*, it has an ornate facade that's listed, but the roof was damaged in a fire in 2011 and the venue is due to reopen in 2016. A few doors away is the **Théâtre du Trianon** (No. 80; tel: 01 44 92 78 00; www. letrianon.fr; pictured), an old operetta and vaudeville hall now used for foot-stomping musicals and accordion fests, as well as rock and *chanson*. Downstairs is its lovely vintage café-bistro, **Le Petit Trianon** (tel: 01 44 92 78 08). **La Cigale** (No. 120; tel: 01 49 25 81 75; www.lacigale.fr) is another glorious old venue with an Art Deco facade and tiered balcony, while next door, laid-back café **La Fourmi** (74 rue des Martyrs; tel: 01 42 64 70 35) is popular before gigs or clubbing at **Le Divan du Monde** (75 rue des Martyrs; tel: 01 42 52 02 46; www.divandumonde.com), a sultry club that has succeeded the

Divan Japonais, immortalised in posters by Toulouse-Lautrec.

As to the famous **Moulin Rouge** (82 boulevard de Clichy; tel: 01 53 09 82 82; www.moulinrouge.fr), it largely plays to coachloads of tourists. For a more fun alternative, try **Chez Michou** (80 rue des Martyrs; tel: 01 46 06 16 04; www.michou.com), where dapper, blue-jacketed Michou comperes a cheeky drag show with a cast of glittering divas.

Pigalle; map D–F4

Live like a modern bohemian in SoPi

What was yesterday's bohemian neighbourhood has become the habitat of the modern 'bobo' or *bourgeois bohème* – though today she is more likely to be eating cheesecake and pushing a buggy than starving in a garret. Climbing like a spine through burgeoning SoPi (southern Pigalle, south of boulevards de Clichy and Rochechouart as opposed to NoPi, on the flanks of Montmartre) is rue des Martyrs. Its lower reaches, pedestrianised on Sunday mornings, are packed with food shops: a *fromagerie* specialising in goat's cheese, a Greek deli, Italian restaurant **Fuxia** and its grocery offshoot, olive

oil emporium **Première Pression Provence** (No. 9), **Aux Produits et Saveurs d'Auvergne** (No. 21) for Auvergnat hams and cheeses, and **Terra Corsa** (No. 42) for Corsican specialities. As so often in Paris, upward mobility can be brilliantly observed in *pâtisseries*. Choose between star baker **Arnaud Delmontel** (No. 39; tel: 01 48 78 29 33) for his Renaissance baguette and cakes flavoured with yuzu, green tea or rhubarb, traditional *pâtissier-chocolatier-glacier* **Sébastien Gaudard** (No.22; tel: 01 71 18 24 70), who previously worked with Fauchon and the legendary Pierre Hermé, and the wholefood hippie ethos of franglais-owned **Rose Bakery** (No. 46; tel: 01 42 82 12 80), where you can eat in or take away carrot cake and crumble, quiches and salads.

Typical of the area's mutation is the **Hôtel Amour** (8 rue de Navarin; tel: 01 48 78 31 80; www.hotel amourparis.fr), gone from seedy hotel to hip, anti-design hangout. The flashing pink neon sign preserves a requisite touch of sleaze, but inside it has artist-created bedrooms and a friendly restaurant in a lovely overgrown courtyard garden.

SoPi: map E3

Discover a Parisian village and a modern eco park at Batignolles

It's intriguing to think that if Monet hadn't exhibited *Impression, Soleil Levant* at the Salon des Refusés in 1874, the Impressionists might have been called the Batignolles School – a reflection of the period when Manet was immortalised in his studio, with Renoir, Bazille, Monet and other friends, in Fantin-Latour's *Un atelier aux Batignolles*. Like neighbouring Montmartre, Batignolles was one of the villages absorbed by Paris in 1860; but it has kept its more workaday social and racial mix and villagey authenticity, a provincial enclave between the din of boulevard des Batignolles, avenue de Clichy and the rue de Rome railway cutting.

Paris populaire, arty Paris and gentrified Paris converge on busy rue des Dames at **Bistro des Dames** (No. 18; tel: 01 45 22 13 42; www.eldoradohotel.fr), where you can eat in the lush garden of bohemian Hôtel Eldorado, and **Les Caves Populaires** (No. 22; tel: 01 53 04 08 32), which draws a crowd of *habitués* for inexpensive wines and simple dishes. Another local hub is the square in front of the pretty neoclassical church Ste-Marie-des-Batignolles, where **L'Endroit** (place du Dr Félix-Lobligeois; tel: 01 42 29 50 00) is a cool drinking haunt by night and a

favourite with families for weekend brunch – before or after a visit to **Square des Batignolles**, with its bandstand, duck pond and giant plane trees. Across rue Cardinet, the **Parc Clichy-Batignolles – Martin-Luther-King** couldn't be more different, a happy aftermath of Paris's failed attempt to score the 2012 Olympics. The area of railway sidings that would have become the Olympic village is instead a new park with an imaginative playground, a challenging skateboard ramp, and an ecological bent: solar panels on a converted forge, a long ditch to collect rainwater, and a pond planted with reeds and irises to clean Seine water for irrigation.

Batignolles: map A5–C4

93

Follow trendsters to Chez Jeannette and the bars of Faubourg St-Denis

Faubourg-St-Denis was once part of a seedy Gare du Nord hinterland. Today, it's at the heart of a fast-evolving bar culture with an underground vibe, where new bars and bistros are thriving amid the Indian restaurants, Arab grocers, halal butchers, Chinese hole-in-the-wall takeaways, African hairdressers and a courtyard mosque. **Chez Jeannette** (47 rue du Fbg-St-Denis; tel: 01 47 70 30 89) has become the unofficial HQ of advertising and design agency types,

musicians and fashion creatives, who gather in an untouched decor of period mouldings, cheerfully ugly copper bar, ghastly wallpaper and kitsch 1940s chandeliers. Up the street, **Le Napoléon** (No. 73; tel: 01 47 70 21 36) has been revamped with a few nods at Napoleon, a fine cheeseburger and a terrace that fills up as soon as the weather perks up. **Le Martel** (3 rue Martel; tel: 01 47 70 67 56) is now a trendy eatery with trad bistro decor, and French and North African dishes.

Some of these spots keep going all day long, others are very much night-time haunts. The stunning Belle Epoque dining room at **La Fidélité** (12 rue de la Fidelité; tel: 01 47 70 19 34; www.lafidelite.com) is fashionable with Parisian night birds; quirky bar **Le Mauri 7** (46 rue du Fbg-St-Denis; tel: 01 44 79 06 42), opposite Chez Jeannette, has vintage record covers and film posters on the walls and a mixed clientele along with affordable drinks and friendly waiters, while **Le Sully** (13 rue du Fbg-St-Denis; tel: 01 77 10 74 70) is a popular, multi-cultural, local hangout offering a similar experience with a charming 'more-shabby-than-chic' ambience.

Faubourg-St-Denis; map G2–H1

Visit a *merveilleuse* in her bathroom at the Petit Hôtel Bourrienne

As is often in Paris, the lovely rue d'Hauteville conceals a treasure: the **Petit Hôtel Bourrienne**, a rare time capsule of the Directoire style of the 1790s – when, in the aftermath of the Revolution, little was built. It belonged first to 19th-century It girl, Fortunée Hamelin, then to Louis-Antoine Fauvelet de Bourrienne, private secretary of Napoleon, and in the 1880s to Charles Tuleu, Balzac's printer, who built the printworks at the end of the garden; his descendants still live in the house today.

Like her friend the Empress Josephine, who hailed from Martinique, Mme Hamelin came from one of the wealthy Caribbean planter families of Santa Dominica. She was one of *les Merveilleuses*, stylish women who introduced the fashion for the low-cut and free-flowing Empire dress (sign of the new frivolity amid the capital's gilded youth after the drama of the Terror), and was notorious for promenading topless – or rather, in transparent muslin – down the Champs-Elysées. The most romantic room of the house? Surely the bathroom, with its marble floor and delicately painted ceiling, where Hamelin would entertain from her bath. But her bedroom is also a gem, decorated with tropical birds and butterflies in memory of the Caribbean.

Bourrienne brought the antechamber, dining room and salon into the Empire style of the time, with classical mouldings, striking ochre and green colour schemes and more, still intact and still very much in use today.

Petit Hôtel Bourrienne; 58 rue d'Hauteville; enquire at the tourist office about opening times; charge; map G2

BASTILLE, BELLEVILLE AND MÉNILMONTANT

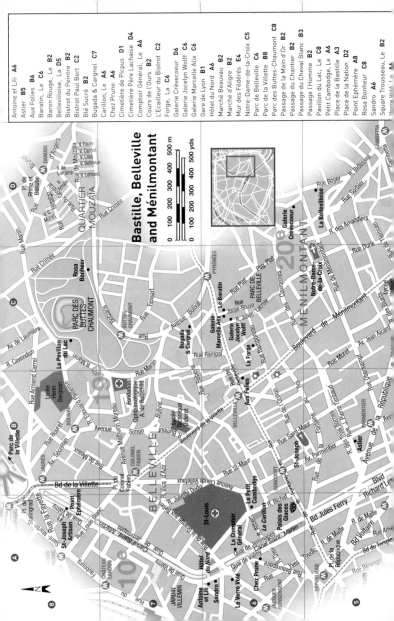

Bastille, Belleville and Ménilmontant

Discover victims of the Terror and an American hero at the Cimetière de Picpus

On a side street not far from Nation, a small cemetery contains the mass grave of thousands of victims of the Terror. While the royals were guillotined on place de la Concorde, by 1794 the guillotine had been set up on the other side of town at place du Trône Renversé (Square of the Overturned Throne) – the new name given to place du Trône before it became the more unifying **place de la Nation** it is today. Here, in just six weeks, 1,306 people were guillotined during the Terror, a last gasp of the Revolution before the fall of Robespierre.

The city of Paris requisitioned the grounds of a former convent nearby and dug two massive communal pits in which to pile the bodies brought in open carts. Later a group of noble families bought the land and created a second cemetery where they could be buried near their guillotined relatives, a select club of aristocratic names that is still a private cemetery today – although as the list of names in the chapel reveals, by far the majority of those guillotined were commoners.

Now run by nuns, the **Cimetière de Picpus** still feels isolated from the rest of the world behind high walls and a long garden. The sites of the two communal graves are marked out, and you can see the walled-up doorway where the carts entered under cover of darkness.

As for the little graveyard of aristocratic French families, its most famous incumbent is more associated with the American Revolution than the French one: the Marquis de Lafayette, who fought in the American War of Independence against the British and drummed up French support. His tomb is draped in the stars and stripes.

Cimetière de Picpus; 35 rue de Picpus; tel: 01 43 44 18 54; Mon–Sat 2–6pm; charge; map D1
Place de la Nation; map D2

Stock up on fresh produce, oysters and banter at the Marché d'Aligre

People cross town for the legendary **rue d'Aligre street market** (Tue–Sun morning), famed for its low prices, stalls laden with fresh produce and stallholders' *tchatche* (banter). The adjoining covered **Marché Beauvau** (Tue–Sat morning and afternoon, Sun morning) is a smarter affair, with a fishmonger, cheese stalls, excellent butcher, wine merchant and a good Italian deli, but it is out on the street where everything happens. Towards the end of the morning prices get even lower as stalls sell off entire crates, and the range of fruit and veg – from tomatoes, artichokes and cherries from France to more exotic produce – gives a touch of rural France meets North African souk. Particularly busy on Sunday mornings when it can be almost impossible to push your way through the crowds, quieter during the week, this is a place to observe a cross-section of Parisians and absorb the repartee.

On the square, a small flea market, the only one in the city centre, is cheerfully junky, with cheap clothes around the edges and a motley mix of old china, second-hand books, jewellery and cutlery in the middle, not to mention a seemingly inexhaustible supply of ghastly vases, although there are always a

few hopefuls looking for a find.

At weekends, the convivial wine bar, **Le Baron Rouge** (1 rue Théophile-Roussel; tel: 01 43 43 14 32), virtually becomes an annex of the market. Wines from all over France are chalked up on blackboards behind the bar, and you can have containers filled from barrels at the front or snack on platters of cheese and charcuterie. In winter an oyster stall sets up on the street on Sunday morning. The smart set breakfast or lunch at pretty Belle Epoque bistro **Square Trousseau** (1 rue Antoine Vollon; tel: 01 43 43 06 00) or pick up *viennoiseries* at fashionable patisserie **Blé Sucré** (7 rue Antoine Vollon; tel: 01 43 40 77 73).

Marché d'Aligre; map B2

Go for a Sunday stroll along the Canal St-Martin, backdrop to chugging barges and the Hôtel du Nord

Tree-lined quays, picturesque locks, a turning bridge and green metal footbridges make the atmospheric Canal St-Martin (map A6–B8) a delightful place to amble. Between some unfortunate modern housing developments, other facades still look as if they could come from a Doisneau photo or Marcel Carné's 1938 film *Hôtel du Nord*, the old hotel now resuscitated as a fashionable bistro. At night there's a grown-up bar scene, as arty locals crowd the laid-back **Chez Prune** (36 rue de Beaurepaire; tel: 01 42 41 30 47) at apéritif time or try to get a table at nearby wine bar-bistro **Le Verre Volé** (67 rue de Lancry; tel: 01 48 03 17 34). It's on Sundays, however, that the canal comes into its own, when the quays are closed to cars, the shops are open, and cyclists, families and dog-walkers turn out for a stroll or to watch the boat traffic chugging through the locks.

The canal was begun by Napoleon in 1802 and completed in 1825 to provide a short cut between the meanders of the Seine and improve the supply of drinking water to the city. It's still used by a surprising amount of boat traffic today, with barges carrying gravel and scrap iron, pleasure boats and boat trips on the canal run by **Canauxrama**

(www.canauxrama.com) and **Paris Canal** (www.pariscanal.com). In 2016 it was dredged and cleaned for the first time in 15 years.

An eclectic crowd piles into the **Hôtel du Nord** (102 quai de Jemmapes; tel: 01 40 40 78 78; www.hoteldunord.org), recently refurbished to look the perfect film-set bistro (the film was actually shot in a studio), with white metro tile walls, Art Deco bar, film lighting and assorted framed photo portraits on the walls. All slightly too good to be true but an animated, cheerful setting for a meal.

A few doors down, behind a graffitied concrete wall, **Le Comptoir Général** (80 quai de Jemmapes; tel: 01 44 88 24 46; www.lecomptoirgeneral.com) has a more alternative mood, a cross between militant ecological group, junk shop and artist's installation, with an overgrown garden and a bric-a-brac interior. There's a bar and restaurant and live music or a DJ several nights a week.

On the bend of the canal, check out the fashions at **Sandro** (93 quai de Valmy); and the colourful clothes and bright global gifts and housewares inside the green, pink and yellow shopfronts of **Antoine et Lili** (No. 95). Just before the Stalingrad lock, **Point Ephémère** (No. 200; tel: 01 40 34 02 48; www.point ephemere.org) is lucky enough to have a terrace stretching along the quayside. A self-proclaimed 'centre of artistic dynamics', it shares the former Point P construction materials' warehouse with a fire station and local organisations; rehearsal studios for music and dance, four artists' studios, a concert hall, exhibition space and a café-restaurant are all to be found here.

On its southern section, between Faubourg-du-Temple and the Bastille, the canal runs under boulevard Richard-Lenoir through a long tunnel, re-emerging just south of place de la Bastille in the Port de l'Arsenal boat marina where it joins the Seine. You can continue your walk along the broad Bassin de la Villette – one of the sites for the annual Paris Plage beach – to the Parc de la Villette (see page 154).

Wind down in the Parc des Buttes-Chaumont, a park with a fantastical bent, and the Quartier Mouzaïa

With the rolling lawns, romantic lake and mature trees of an 'English-style' garden, the picturesque **Parc des Buttes-Chaumont** was one of the new parks laid out by Napoleon III in the 1860s in his mission to bring fresh air to the people. In fact, the park is an amusing mixture of natural and fake, created over the site of old gypsum quarries that proved just perfect for conjuring up a dramatic landscape – including a lake, a craggy island crowned by a classical temple, a dramatic ravine complete with suspension bridge and a cave with fake stalactites.

You'll find all the facilities of a good local park too: puppet shows, pony rides and playgrounds for kids, plenty of lawns for lounging on, and two Belle Epoque pavilions containing restaurant **Le Pavillon du Lac** and convivial 'restaurant-guinguette' (an open-air dance hall) **Rosa Bonheur**.

Take a look at the rest of the district too. The Haussmannian apartments overlooking the park have become highly desirable, while across rue de Crimée, the **Quartier Mouzaïa** exudes a charm that is endearingly provincial. The triangle of tightly packed leafy streets – such as Villa Amalia, Villa de Lorraine, Villa Bellevue and Villa Claude Monet – which run off rue Hidalgo, rue du Général-Brunet and rue Mouzaïa, was built in 1901 like a little garden suburb to provide affordable housing for local workers. The houses couldn't be more than two storeys high because they were built over old gypsum quarries, in contrast to the 1960s tower blocks of place des Fêtes. The triangle is now a sought-after oasis of little brick houses and front gardens overflowing with wisteria and roses.

Parc des Buttes-Chaumont; entrances rue Bozaris, rue Manin; www.paris.fr; May–Aug daily 7am–10pm, Sept 7am–9pm, Oct–Apr 7am–8pm; free; map C8

Relish a timeless bistro experience in the vicinity of the Bastille

Ask most Parisians where they really like going out to eat, and it's not the grand occasion temples but their favourite Paris bistro, offering good food and good value in a casual, friendly atmosphere.

Astier has stayed in the 1950s of painted pine skirtings and red and white napkins, but has also seamlessly changed hands from Monsieur and Madame Astier to a young team. You'll find modern seasonal dishes alongside eternal favourites, like the pickled herrings you help yourself to from a terracotta dish and a very tipsy rum baba. The wine list is renowned and the diners eclectic.

East of the Bastille, rue Paul Bert has become a foodie enclave led by the **Bistrot Paul Bert**, a convivial if slightly cliquey rendez-vous for the area's young *bobos* (hipsters). Food is French trad, well done and the gigantic *côte de bœuf* served for two with chunky 'peasant' chips is a treat. The same team also runs next door fish restaurant **L'Ecailleur du Bistrot**.

The cheerful all-day **Bistrot du Peintre** (pictured) has a gorgeous listed Art Nouveau decor of sinuous woodwork and tiled figures representing spring and summer. It's busy lunch and dinner for its Auvergnat and southwestern specialities, peppered daily with cosmopolitan suggestions such as courgette tatin with tomato sorbet.

Astier, 44 rue Jean-Pierre-Timbaud; tel: 01 43 57 16 35; www.restaurant-astier.com; L and D daily; map B5
Bistrot Paul Bert, 18 rue Paul-Bert; tel: 01 43 72 24 01; L and D Tue–Sat; map C2
Bistrot du Peintre, 116 avenue Ledru-Rollin; tel: 01 47 00 34 39; www.bistrotdu peintre.com; L and D daily; map B2

Go arty in the heights of Belleville

Like many of the poorer fringes of the city, Belleville has been endlessly settled by waves of immigrants: Parisians displaced by the demolition of the slums, peasants fresh from the land, later Arabs, Africans and Chinese, Jews and Muslims, more recently, artists and designers – and all of them seem to cram into **Aux Folies** (8 rue de Belleville; pictured), a frantic bar with a crazy maze of neon on the ceiling.

This is the *Paris populaire* where singer Edith Piaf was born, literally in the street outside No. 72, and where the old tenements and steep stairways familiar from the classic children's film *The Red Balloon* now mix with Chinese restaurants and modern housing projects. Beneath the **Parc de Belleville**, which descends in terraces between rue Piat and rue Jouye-Rouve, **La Forge**

(25 rue Ramponneau), an old key factory, began as an artists' squat in 1991 and is now home to around 20 artists who rent studios from the municipality. Other studios can be visited in the **Belleville open studios** (www.ateliers-artistes-belleville.org) each May.

Recently a cluster of interesting art galleries have set up here too, like **Galerie Jocelyn Wolff** (78 rue Julien-Lacroix; tel: 01 42 03 05 65); **Galerie Crèvecœur** (9 rue des Cascades; tel: 09 54 57 31 26) and **Galerie Marcelle Alix** (4 rue Jouye-Rouve; tel: 09 50 04 16 80), which squeezes installations and performances into a tiny shopfront space opposite cult bistro **Le Baratin** (No. 3; tel: 01 43 49 39 70), a shabby-chic favourite of superchefs and gourmets; while **Bugada & Cargnel** (7-9 rue de l'Equerre; tel: 01 42 71 72 73) holds shows in a 1930s Citroën garage.

A touch of the area's old militancy remains in the cool, edgy programming at **La Bellevilloise** (19 rue Boyer; tel: 01 46 36 07 07; www.labellevilloise.com), a pioneering cooperative founded in 1887 turned multi-disciplinary arts centre with restaurant.

Parc de Belleville; map C6

Explore the alleyways of Faubourg St-Antoine, where furniture craftsmen alternate with media folk

Faubourg-St-Antoine, and not Bastille, used to be the name given not just to a street but to this entire district, synonymous with furniture making ever since the 15th century when furniture makers were allowed to set up workshops on land belonging to the Abbaye de St-Antoine, free of the guild restrictions for craftsmen within the city wall. In the 17th and 18th centuries, the finest cabinet makers in Europe settled along here. A distinctive architecture developed where, behind street facades with their lodgings, doorways give way to long workshop-lined alleys bearing mysterious names such as Passage de la Tête Brûlée (Burnt Head Passage) and Passage de l'Ours (Bear Passage) – with a carved bear over the entrance.

Today, most of the furniture showrooms along Faubourg-St-Antoine itself have been replaced by the likes of Nike, Etam and Gap. Poke through doorways on the Faubourg and neighbouring rue de la Roquette and rue de Charonne during the week (some close at weekends) however, and there are still a surprising number of cabinet makers at work behind the scenes, though many workshops have been colonised by a breed of more contemporary creatives: photographers, radio stations, etc.

Almost on the corner of place de la Bastille, **Passage du Cheval Blanc** leads through a series of cobbled courtyards before emerging through Cité Parchappe. **Passage du Chantier** still has furniture outlets with old shopfronts and salesmen who try to lure you in off the street. **Passage de la Main d'Or** contains a Corsican restaurant and a fringe theatre, while **Passage Lhomme** (between rue de Charonne and avenue Ledru-Rollin) is a creeper-clad dream of cottages, wooden shopfronts and painted shutters.

Faubourg St-Antoine; map A3–E1

Seek out Honoré, Théodore, Edith and a raft of French stars at Père Lachaise cemetery

There's an undeniable kudos to being buried at Père Lachaise, with its winding cobbled lanes lined with family sepulchres in the form of Greek temples and Byzantine churches, obelisks, Gothic chapels and Egyptian pyramids, like houses in a city of the dead.

One of four cemeteries created after the old overcrowded city churchyards had been transferred to the Catacombes (see page 143), the cemetery opened in 1804 on land that had belonged to the Jesuits and named after Louis XIV's confessor Père Lachaise. Initially, Parisians considered it too far out of town and were reluctant to be buried here, so in 1817 playwright Molière, fabulist La Fontaine and the fanciful supposed tomb of medieval lovers Abélard and Héloise were moved here to make it fashionable – bringing with them a desirability that has never waned. Concessions are now hard to come by but the cemetery remains a preferred resting place for French artists, actors and intellectuals, which have recently included singer Mano Solo and mime artist Marcel Marceau.

Père Lachaise offers a snapshot of French intellectual and political history, with countless writers, artists, actresses, scientists, generals and politicians buried here (among them Delacroix, Pissarro, Ingres, Colette, Rossini, Bizet, Proust and actress Sarah Bernhardt). Almost all of Napoleon's generals are here. Egyptologist Champollion is appropriately commemorated by an obelisk, painter Théodore Géricault has reliefs of some of his most famous works, including the *Raft of the Medusa*, Honoré de Balzac is buried with his beloved Comtesse Hanska under a bronze bust of himself, and Allan Kardec, founder of spiritism, is remembered by what looks like a prehistoric dolmen.

Some people take a very studious approach to visiting the cemetery, devotedly poring over maps to track down the famous names; but it is equally rewarding to let yourself wander at random to make your own discoveries among the forgotten poets, inventors, administrators, singers and radicals who helped shape Paris in the 19th century, or to simply admire this incredible outdoor gallery of funerary art. Sculptures include generals on horses, seafarers and their ships, mourning nymphs, stern portraits, weeping draped figures and the side-by-side bronze effigies of Croce-Spinelli and Sivel, who died in a ballooning accident at 8,600 metres (28,215 ft) on 15 April 1875. Soaring over everything, like a Greek temple on stilts, is the tallest monument in the cemetery, the 35 metre (115ft)-high monument to a certain Princesse Elisabeth de Davidoff.

The northern sector of the cemetery is less romantic with its geometrical layout but it does contain some cult tombs that draw devoted pilgrims, including that of Jim Morrison, Edith Piaf buried under a simple polished marble slab next to her last husband Theophanis Lamboukas, and Oscar Wilde, with a Cubist nude sculpted by Jacob Epstein, smothered in lipstick kisses.

Dotted around the cemetery are memorials to the Paris Commune, to municipal workers, to the Spanish Civil War and World War II deportees. Radical working-class Ménilmontant was one of the last pockets of resistance during the Paris Commune of 1871 which, in *la Semaine sanglante* (Bloody Week), culminated in a last stand in the cemetery: 147 Communards were shot by Versaillais troops in the north-east corner against the wall now known as the Mur des Fédérés and buried in a common

grave, a symbol of workers' struggle for liberation.

Cimetière du Père-Lachaise; boulevard du Ménilmontant; tel: 01 55 25 82 10; www.paris.fr; Mon–Fri 8am–6pm, Sat 8.30am–6pm, Sun 9am–6pm, winter until 5.30pm; free; map D4

LATIN QUARTER, ST-GERMAIN AND SEINE

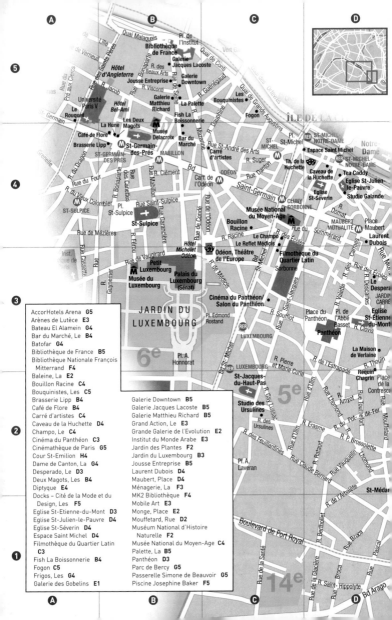

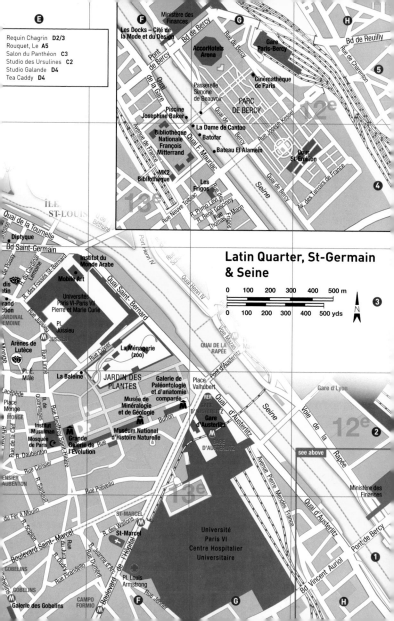

E

Requin Chagrin **D2/3**
Rouquet, Le **A5**
Salon du Panthéon **C3**
Studio des Ursulines **C2**
Studio Galande **D4**
Tea Caddy **D4**

Ministère des Finances

Les Docks – Cité de la Mode et du Design

AccorHotels Arena

Gare Paris-Bercy

Bd de Reuilly

Cinémathèque de Paris

Passerelle Simone de Beauvoir

PARC DE BERCY

Piscine Josephine Baker

La Dame de Canton

Batofar

Bibliothèque Nationale François Mitterrand

Bateau El Alamein

Cour St-Émilion

Seine

MK2 Bibliothèque

Les Frigos

12e

13e

Av. des Terroirs de France

ÎLE ST-LOUIS

Diptyque

Bd Saint-Germain

Latin Quarter, St-Germain & Seine

0 100 200 300 400 500 m
0 100 200 300 400 500 yds

N

3

Institut du Monde Arabe

Mobile Art

Université Paris VI-Paris VII Pierre et Marie Curie

Pl. Jussieu

La Ménagerie (zoo)

QUAI DE LA RÂPÉE

Gare d'Lyon

Arènes de Lutèce

La Baleine

JARDIN DES PLANTES

Galerie de Paléontologie et d'anatomie comparée

Place Valhubert

Pl. E. Mâle

Musée de Minéralogie et de Géologie

Place Monge

Institut Musulman Mosquée de Paris

Grande Galerie de l'Évolution

Museum National d'Histoire Naturelle

Gare d'Austerlitz

12e

see above

ENSIER AUBENTON

St-Marcel

Université Paris VI Centre Hospitalier Universitaire

Ministère des Finances

13e

Boulevard Saint-Marcel

Pl. Louis Armstrong

Pont de Bercy

GOBELINS

Galerie des Gobelins

CAMPO FORMIO

1

Spot ostriches and dinosaurs at the Jardin des Plantes

You could easily spend a whole family day out in the **Jardin des Plantes**, home to a botanical garden, natural history museum and zoo, plus all the playgrounds and ice cream stalls of a local park. The place is also home to an active scientific research institute with an illustrious past: botanist Sébastien Vaillant proved the principle of pollination and plant sexuality here in 1718 with a pistachio tree still in the garden, while physics professor Henri Becquerel demonstrated radiation from uranium in the laboratory in 1896, a heritage reflected in the nearby streets which are almost all named after eminent scientists (Buffon, Cuvier, Linné, Daubenton, etc).

The gardens originated as the royal medicinal garden and botanical school of Louis XIII, open to the public since 1640. At first sight they resemble a typical formal garden with planted quadrangles and avenues of trees creating a perspective up to the natural history museum. But they also constitute an incredible botanical reserve of more than 6,000 plant species and numerous historic trees.

Particularly interesting is the **Alpine garden** with rockeries and peat bogs of mountain species. The **botanical school gardens** present temperate zones from around the globe, the **roseraie** has 390 varieties of roses modern and old, and a historic **labyrinth** spirals up a hill to a picturesque wrought-iron gazebo. Even the model of the stegosaurus by the rue Buffon entrance has been surrounded by the appropriate 'archaic' plants, such as ferns and horsetails.

The **ecological garden** was created in 1932, well before ecology was newsworthy, to preserve the different natural habitats of the Ile de France. A wilderness of a bird and bee garden is home to a log cabin bee house, while the imposing 19th-century **greenhouses** have recently reopened following restoration and showcase tropical ecosystems.

Scattered around the park are the assorted departments of the Muséum National d'Histoire Naturelle. Most spectacular is the **Grande Galerie de l'Evolution**, sitting like a palace at the end of the central gardens, and brilliantly renovated to display stuffed animals by habitat in the central nave. Marine animals and Arctic species occupy the ground floor, a procession of giraffes, zebras and antelopes steps out across the savannah on the first floor, and birds hang suspended as you rise up between them in glass lifts. The star curiosity is Louis XV's Indian rhinoceros, an early masterpiece of taxidermy, though slightly bulky as an old table was used for the frame.

The park also contains a newly reopened mineralogy pavilion, containing a spectacular array of minerals, meteorites and crystals, and paleontology and anatomy pavilions.

La Ménagerie is a small zoo founded in 1794 when the former royal menagerie was transferred here from Versailles. Winding paths bring you to a flamingo pool, 19th-century aviary, art deco monkey house, the ostrich paddock, wooden climbing frames where red pandas lounge and the reptarium, home to scary snakes and spiders. During the siege of Paris; hungry Parisians were forced to eat the zoo's inhabitants and it became fashionable to say you had just tasted lion.

Take a break at the snack and ice cream stand near the entrance to the Ménagerie or go for a full-scale lunch at **La Baleine** (tel: 01 40 79 80 72), with an interior inspired by the whale skeleton from the anatomy gallery, and plenty of outdoor tables.

Jardins des Plantes; Place Valhubert (other entrances 57 rue Cuvier, 2 rue Bouffon, 36 rue Geoffroy-St-Hilaire); tel: 01 40 79 56 01; www.mnhn.fr; park daily summer 7.30am–8pm, winter 8am–5.30pm, Alpine garden hours vary, zoo daily 9am–6pm, museums and greenhouses Wed–Mon 10am–6pm; charge for zoo, greenhouses and museums; map F2

Decipher a medieval allegory at Cluny

The *Lady and the Unicorn* tapestry cycle is one of the great masterpieces of medieval art, an endlessly fascinating allegory of love and the senses that abounds in charm with its gentle-looking lion and smiling unicorn against the millefiore background sprinkled with rabbits and flowers. Five tapestries represent the senses: in one the lady eats from a bowl of sweetmeats (taste), in another she holds up a mirror to the unicorn who gazes at his reflection (sight), she plays a small organ (sound), holds a penant and the unicorn's horn (touch) and makes a wreath of flowers (smell). In the mysterious sixth, she stands before a tent, with the words *à mon seul désir* (to my only desire) woven into it. Opinions vary as to whether the lady is placing her necklace in the casket held by her maid or removing it, and whether it signifies love and desire or, rather, the renunciation of worldly senses.

You could easily sit for hours in the circular room where the tapestries are displayed absorbing the detail, but there are plenty of other good reasons to visit the **Musée National du Moyen-Age** (often known as Cluny). The 15th-century Gothic townhouse of the powerful abbots of Cluny makes a perfect setting for medieval works of art, with an intimate human scale that suits the intricately worked pieces. Moreover, the building combines with by far the most substantial Roman remains in Paris – the 1st-century Thermes de Cluny baths complex. The heads of the kings of Judah from Notre-Dame, knocked off during the Revolution and rediscovered in the 1970s, can be admired against a backdrop of soaring Roman masonry.

Musée National du Moyen-Age; 5 place Paul-Painlevé; tel: 01 53 73 78 16; www.musee-moyenage.fr; Wed–Mon 9.15am–5.45pm; charge; map C4

Marvel at the unfurling palm tree column inside Eglise St-Séverin

The leering gargoyles may look suitably Gothic but inside **Eglise St-Séverin** (rue des Prêtres-St-Séverin), the overwhelming impression is one of space and light. The church, dating from the 13th to 15th centuries, has five naves and a forest of slender columns allowing you to see right through to the double ambulatory with its famous twisted 'palm tree' column from which all the ribs flow into a complex web of vaulting overhead. Artist Robert Delaunay was so fascinated by the column that he painted it frequently from 1909 to 1912. As you leave, take a look at the adjacent charnel house.

St-Séverin is at the heart of the Paris district that has most kept its medieval character, even if now filled with cheap Greek restaurants, jazz cellars and souvenir shops rather than the medieval scholars of yore. The buildings come in a comfortably eclectic mix – a 1930s Art Deco hotel, fine 18th-century facades and ancient tenements with sloping walls – often built over much older cellars, such as the **Caveau de la Huchette** jazz club (5 rue de la Huchette; tel: 01 43 26 65 05; www.caveaudelahuchette.fr), where the vaulted medieval cellars provided a hangout for Rosicrucians and Revolutionaries.

Across rue St-Jacques, ancient Roman road and pilgrimage route to Compostela, is the small **Eglise St-Julien-le-Pauvre**, built in the 12th century over a Merovingian necropolis. Long used for rowdy university assemblies, it now belongs to the Melkite Greek Catholic church; icons grace the iconostasis and walls amid medieval carved capitals.

Not quite as ancient, but a monument in its own right, is the robinia tree in the adjoining garden, Paris's oldest tree planted in 1602 and now propped up by a concrete buttress. Across the street, the **Tea Caddy** (14 rue St-Julien-le-Pauvre; tel: 01 43 54 15 56; www.the-tea-caddy.com) has been serving très British cream teas, complete with willow pattern china, since 1928.

Eglise St-Séverin; map D4

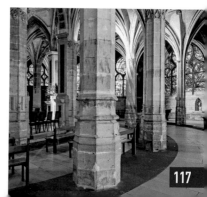

Pay homage to great men on place du Panthéon

Crowning the Montagne-Sainte-Geneviève, the **Panthéon** forms one of the grand set pieces of Parisian architecture – its vast dome a landmark that can be spotted from all over the city, and its pedimented front forming a grand perspective from the Jardin du Luxembourg. Begun in 1764, the building, designed by Soufflot, was originally commissioned as a shrine for the relics of Saint Geneviève, patron saint of Paris, but the Revolution intervened and it was converted into a shrine to France's great men instead.

The vast interior is a very pure example of classical architecture designed on a Greek cross plan: colonnades with crisply carved Corinthian capitals and coffered dome, where Foucault hung his pendulum in 1851 to demonstrate the rotation of the Earth. Murals by Cabanal, Bonnat, Puvis de Chavannes and others illustrate episodes from Saint Geneviève's life; but the white marble sculpture *La Convention Nationale*, at the back, is defiantly republican, depicting the figure of Marianne brandishing a sword, surrounded by groups of soldiers. From April to October, you can climb up to the dome for a 360° view over the city.

France's great men (and three women: Marie Curie and the symbolic remains of two Resistance heroines – a fourth, the wife of chemist Marcellin Berthelot, is buried here with her husband at his request) rest in the labyrinthine barrel-vaulted crypt. It's the place to pay homage to some great writers, philosophers, scientists and forgotten statesmen and an intriguing insight into the nation's self-image: the wooden tomb of Rousseau and that of Voltaire, Victor Hugo, Emile Zola and Alexandre Dumas (moved here by Jacques Chirac), not to mention Léon Gambetta's heart.

Panthéon; place du Panthéon; tel: 01 44 32 18 00; www.pantheon.monuments-nationaux.fr; daily 10am–6.30pm, winter until 6pm; charge; map D3

Buy from producers at Marché Monge or Maubert and then picnic in a Roman arena

Eavesdrop on a few conversations and you soon realise just how much Parisians talk about food, with the local market essential both for stocking up and as a social rendez-vous at weekends. It's typical that although the Latin Quarter has three markets within a ten-minute walk of each other, each has its own afficionados. **Place Monge** (Wed, Fri, Sun 7am–2.30pm) is a great reminder that there are still market gardeners in the Ile de France and neighbouring Picardy, with producers of apples and pears, organic veg, honey and honey cakes, plus a stall of mountain hams and cheeses, fish direct from Boulogne, usually a wine producer or two, and hot roast chicken, *choucroute garnie* and Lebanese snacks if you want an instant picnic. **Place Maubert** (Tue, Thur, Sat 7am–2.30pm) has been a market for centuries – at one point

even a *marché aux mégots*, where tramps resold tobacco gleaned from fag ends. Now it's rather upmarket and pricier than Monge, with organic produce, foie gras and olive oil stalls, and excellent cheese shop Laurent Dubois at the back of the square. It's mainly food on Saturdays, while fashion and tribal art tip the balance during the week. Not officially a market but a food-shopping street, picturesque **Rue Mouffetard** (Tue–Sat morning and afternoon, Sun morning) has a more touristy feel, especially on Sunday when often accompanied by street musicians. But it has good cheese and other shops.

Picnic on your finds in the **Arènes de Lutèce** (47 rue Monge), the surprising remains of Paris's Roman arena, which once seated 17,000 for gladiatorial combats.

Place Monge; map E2

Watch tapestry weavers at work at the Manufacture des Gobelins

Since the magnificent **Galerie des Gobelins** reopened in 2007, it's put on some impressive shows on themes ranging from modern design to Renaissance tapestries. The gallery is however much more than a museum: it's the frontispiece for a working tapestry factory, whose weaving workshops you can visit. Tapestries are still made painstakingly by hand on big vertical looms just as they were in the factory's previous incarnation as the Manufacture Royale des Tapisseries – founded by Colbert, Louis XIV's minister of finance, in 1662, on the site where Jehan Gobelin set up his dye workshops by the Bièvre river in the 15th century – and sometimes in the very same buildings. In fact most of the original 17th-century architecture remains, including the old laboratory where dyes were mixed. All the wools are still hand-dyed here and as many as 170 different shades employed in a single tapestry.

The factory is now a state institution. Most of the tapestries are created in collaboration with contemporary artists, generally for government ministries or embassies (places that can wait four or five years). It's impressive to see how the weavers work from an original photograph or painting, painstakingly matching colours and translating a small image into wool, blown up to 3–4 metres/10–13ft high. Strike lucky and you may time it right to witness a *tombée de métier* – the moment when the finished tapestry is finally cut off the loom and first hung up to view.

Manufacture des Gobelins, 42 avenue des Gobelins; tel: 01 44 08 53 49; www.mobilier national.culture.gouv.fr; gallery (during exhibitions) Tue–Sun 11am–6pm, visits (tel: 0892 68 46 94) Sat 2.30pm and 4pm; charge; map E1

Follow Orwell and Hemingway to literary haunts on the Mouff'

Ever since Rabelais caroused at the Pomme de Pin on place de la Contrescarpe, the **Mouffetard district** has drawn partying Sorbonne students and writers in search of inspiration. The area is still marked by the expats who fuelled a literary effervescence here between the wars, drawn by inexpensive restaurants and cheap lodgings. Today **Café Delmas** and **Café La Contrescarpe** compete with their pavement terraces, **Le Requin Chagrin** attracts a studenty set, and a painted sign of **Au Nègre Joyeux** is still visible over a small supermarket. George Orwell lived in a seedy hotel in rue du Pot-de-Fer in 1928–9 while he worked as *plongeur* (washer up) at the Hôtel Lotti, gathering material for *Down and Out in Paris and London*, – in which the street is called rue du Coq d'Or: 'a ravine of tall, leprous houses, lurching towards one another in queer attitudes, as though they had all been frozen in the act of collapse. All the houses were hotels and packed to the tiles with lodgers, mostly Poles, Arabs and Italians. At the foot of the hotels were tiny bistros, where you could be drunk for the equivalent of a shilling.' The hotels have gone but the street is still filled with inexpensive restaurants.

In 1921, James Joyce completed *Ulysses* while staying in an apartment at 71 rue du Cardinal-Lemoine, lent to him by his translator, Valéry Larbaud (only the rural-looking lane leading to the courtyard is visible from the street). The book, which had been banned for obscenity in Britain and the US, was published first in Paris – in rue de l'Odéon – in a tiny edition by Sylvia Beach in February 1922. Also in 1922, a young Ernest Hemingway and his wife Hadley lodged in a flat at 74 rue du Cardinal-Lemoine, later moving round the corner to 39 rue Descartes, the building where poet Paul Verlaine died in 1896. It is now a restaurant called **La Maison de Verlaine**.

Rue Mouffetard; map D2

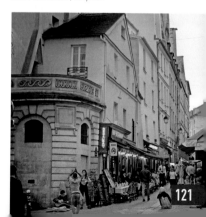

Join St-Germain café society

When it comes to boulevard St-Germain there's only one question to be asked: are you Flore or are you Magots? Paris's two most famous cafés, **Café de Flore** (172 boulevard St-Germain; tel: 01 45 48 55 26) and **Les Deux Magots** (6 place St-Germain-des-Prés; tel: 01 45 48 55 25) still draw the (g)literati – now mingled with the international jet set and tourists. The legendary duo form an intriguingly self-perpetuating literary tradition, still favoured by writers for interviews and rendezvous, each one awarding its own literary prize. It boils down to a question of taste: the Deux Magots with its wooden statues of the two magots or magi (wise men), its regulars for weekend breakfast, and shielded terrace; or, the Flore (pictured), with its red banquettes and Art Deco lights, and service with

a dry sense of humour delivered by imperturbable waiters in waistcoats and white aprons. The Flore drew the Surrealists in the 1920s, Sartre and De Beauvoir during the war when they came here to write by the warm stove, singers Juliette Gréco and Serge Gainsbourg, now succeeded by a new generation. To-day's *germanopratines* (St-Germain's female residents) favour the interior, lunch regulars prize the first floor.

Meanwhile, politicians go for stuffier **Brasserie Lipp** (151 boulevard St-Germain) across the street. **Le Rouquet** (No. 188; map A5) is a temple to 1950s neon and formica, while young trendies kiss cheeks on the terrace at **Le Bar du Marché** (75 rue de Seine), with its vantage point over the rue de Buci food shops.

Boulevard and Place St-Germain; map B4

Pick up the best of modern design in the St-Germain gallery district

Rue de Seine, at the heart of the St-Germain gallery district, has become a treasure trove for sought-after modern design classics, designed in the 1940s and 1950s by avant-garde architects. At **Galerie Downtown** (No.18; tel: 01 46 33 82 41), François Laffanour shows contemporary designers like Ron Arad, Gaetano Pesce and the sculptural balancing acts of Korean Byung Hoon Choi; as well as 1950s design classics, such as Serge Mouille's spider-like black metal lamps and the output of Jean Prouvé.

Galerie Matthieu Richard (No. 34; tel: 01 56 24 44 87) specialises in the pierced metal furniture by Mathieu Matégot. **Jousse Entreprise** (No. 18; tel: 01 53 82 13 60) is an expert on Jean Prouvé, and here you might find sections of Prouvé's innovative prefabricated buildings as well as his furniture, along with designers such as Charlotte Perriand, Pierre Paulin and ceramicist Georges Jouve. At **Galerie Jacques Lacoste** (No. 12; tel: 01 40 20 41 82), the predilection is for Jean Royère, a fashionable decorator of the 1940s.

Carré d'Artistes (60 rue St-André-des-Arts; tel: 01 43 29 63 69; www.carredartistes.com), inspired by Andy Warhol's belief that art should be for everyone, specialises in contemporary artworks by some 600 international artists with prices starting from as little as €75.

For lunch, gallerists decamp to **La Palette** (No. 43; tel: 01 43 26 68 15), the archetypal Art Nouveau artist's café, with palettes hanging over the bar and pavement tables for a steak tartare or croque monsieur; or to cheerful bistro and wine bar **Fish La Boissonnerie** (No. 69; tel: 01 43 54 34 69; map B4), set behind the mosaic shopfront of a former *poissonnerie* (fishmonger).

St Germain; map B5

Take a pew in one of the iconic green chairs of the Jardin du Luxembourg to watch Parisians at play

The classic Parisian park with sculptures, a bandstand and all the activities and facilities for garden-starved apartment dwellers, the **Jardin du Luxembourg** is not so much old-fashioned as timeless: a palimpsest of Parisian life, with its pétanque pitches, tennis courts, cafés, playgrounds and sandpits, go carts, pony rides, cast-iron carousel, and a circular pond where generations of children have hired toy sailing boats in summer. One thing the Luxembourg gardens has made its own is the green metal Luxembourg chair, a desirable attribute for practising the très Parisian art of people-watching.

The Jardin began life as the private gardens of the Palais du Luxembourg (now the Sénat), built in 1614 in Renaissance Mannerist style inspired by the Pitti Palace in Florence for Marie de Médicis, when she no longer wanted to live in the Louvre after the assassination of Henri IV. There are gravel paths and lawns, bee hives where you can take courses in beekeeping and heritage collections of neatly espaliered apple and pear trees. The gardens are also a mini museum of sculpture, with the white stone figures of the queens of France providing a splendid evocation of fashion down the centuries and a sort of proto-feminist recognition of obscure women. Most dramatic is the Médicis fountain modelled on Renaissance grottoes, a giant cyclops looming over the romantically gloomy carp pool.

Jardin du Luxembourg; place Edmond-Rostand/boulevard St-Michel/rue Guynemer/rue de Vaugirard; www.senat.fr; daily, times vary between Dec–Jan 8.15am–4.45pm and June–mid July 7.30am–9.30pm; free; map B3

Touch down in Zaha Hadid's pavilion at the Institut du Monde Arabe

The **Institut du Monde Arabe** may be a centre for Arabic culture but it is equally a destination for anyone interested in modern architecture, all the more so since Jean Nouvel's original building was joined in 2011 by Zaha Hadid's flying-saucer-like **Mobile Art** gallery. Looking like a shiny white doughnut that has just landed on the forecourt by the institute, Anglo-Iraqi architect Zaha Hadid's sleek white structure was originally designed for Chanel as a travelling gallery, made out of lightweight panels that could be packed up in crates and shipped around the world. Reconstructed here for temporary exhibitions, its distorted torus form is a sculpture in its own right, with an interior that doesn't seem to have a vertical wall in sight.

Next door, the original institute was one of the most successful of President Mitterrand's *Grands Projets*, a brilliant modern interpretation of Arab architecture in glass and steel. Financed by 19 Arab countries, Nouvel called it 'a hinge between two cultures and two histories': one side with complex, articulated steel shutters recalling the carved wood screens of traditional Arab buildings, the other glazed to reflect the cityscape across the Seine. The Institut has a library, shop, cinema and auditorium. On the first floor, the museum explores Islamic heritage, through beautiful tiles and ceramics, embroidered fabrics, scientific instruments and Persian miniatures. Take one of the glass lifts to Lebanese restaurant Le Zyriab, with an astonishing view of Paris from the roof terrace.

Institut du Monde Arabe, 1 rue des Fossés-Saint-Bernard; tel: 01 40 51 38 38; www.imarabe.org; Tue–Thu 10am–6pm, Fri until 9.30pm, Sat–Sun until 7pm; charge; map E3

Go aquatic in the new east with a dip in a floating swimming pool and nautical nightlife to follow

The four L-shaped towers of the **Bibliothèque Nationale François Mitterrand**, France's new national library, herald the Paris Seine Rive Gauche development area, dubbed the 'new Latin Quarter', growing on the place of old railway sidings and warehouses. Despite its aura of big statement architecture as the last of Mitterrand's *Grands Projets*, the library designed by Dominique Perrault is actually a building that works better on the inside than out, with a glazed corridor running all round the central well – which contains an imported pine wood – reading rooms open to all, and temporary exhibitions.

Unlike many new districts mainly devoted to business, here there's a surprisingly successful mix: a university, residential, business and even entertainment district, where new buildings are interspersed with parks and traces of the area's industrial past. During the week it buzzes with students and office workers, at weekends it's more likely to be cinema-goers heading for the 14-screen **MK2 Bibliothèque** multiplex.

From the library, spot the artfully graffitied concrete of **Les Frigos** (rue des Frigos; www.les-frigos.com), old refrigerated warehouses, home to more than 200 artists, musicians, photographers and craftspeople; visit in the annual *portes ouvertes* (open house) in May. Further along, the Moulins de Paris flour mills have had a stylish conversion into a new university library, while along the quays, the 1890s compressed air building with modern extension is now an architecture school.

Across the river

The **Passerelle Simone de Beauvoir**, Paris's 37th and newest bridge, was ingeniously designed by Austrian architect Dietmar Feichtinger to give you a choice of routes – from the deck of the Bibliothèque Nationale or down at quay level, above or below – to the **Parc de Bercy** across the river, a modern park created where wine used to be brought in on barges (although the area has also gained an ominous association with taxes since the **Ministry of Finance** moved here). The strange grass-covered pyramid is the **AccorHotels Arena** (formerly known as Palais Omnisports de Paris-Bercy) indoor stadium used for sports and rock concerts, then there's the **Cinémathèque de Paris** repertory cinema and film museum (originally designed by Frank Gehry as the American Centre) and **Cour St-Emilion**, old wine warehouses converted into wine bars, cafés and boutiques. Map G4–5

Behind the library, the broad avenue de France has been laid out, a frontier between brave new world and old Paris. Spot the homage to Astérix's creator in rue René-Goscinny, where speech bubbles adorn lampposts, and the Biopark, its buildings covered in a tangle of climbing plants.

On the waterfront, **Les Docks – Cité de la Mode et du Design** (Quai d'Austerlitz; www.citemode design.fr), housed in former warehouses, is the new HQ of the Institut Français de la Mode (French Fashion Institute) and has a museum dedicated to cartoons and video games; there are also bars, nightclubs and restaurants including a summer terrace on its undulating green roof. South east of the library, the Port de la Gare has become another new entertainment hub, with the **Piscine Josephine Baker** (tel: 01 56 61 96 50; www.paris.fr), a floating swimming pool with a retractable roof and sunbathing deck in summer, and a cluster of lively music bars. Red steel lighthouse ship **Batofar** (tel: 09 71 25 50 61; www.batofar.org) is one of Paris's best clubs with a bar and restaurant. **La Dame de Canton** (www.damedecanton.com) puts on eclectic live music and DJs in a Chinese sailing junk, while purple **Bateau El Alamein** (www.bateauel alamein.com) veers more towards chanson and jazz.

Bibliothèque Nationale François Mitterrand; quai François Mauriac; tel: 01 53 79 59 59; Tue–Sat 10am–8pm, Sun 1–7pm, closed 2 weeks Sept; charge; map F4

INVALIDES AND MONTPARNASSE

Invalides and Montparnasse

View the giants of Impressionism in the setting of a converted railway station at the Musée d'Orsay

You could hardly find a better setting for Impressionist paintings than the converted Gare d'Orsay train station, with its grandiose coffered vault and sculpture displayed where trains once pulled in. The Impressionists were artists of the steam age, inspired by the modernity of train travel (Monet's *Gare St-Lazare*), dance halls (Renoir), the ballet (Degas) and watersports, and taking the train to flit to the beach at Trouville.

The collection contains an astonishing hit list of Impressionism: five of Monet's *Rouen Cathedral* series, views of the garden at Giverny,

Manet's *Déjeuner sur l'herbe* and *L'Olympia*, Degas's racehorses, ballerina pastels and bronzes, before Post-Impressionist icons by Cézanne, Gauguin and Van Gogh. But the collection running from 1848 to 1906 is much broader than Impression – fortunately so, as the Impressionist galleries tend to be the most crowded – also taking in the decorative arts, sculpture and early photography as well as more painting. Don't miss Daumier's wonderful caricature heads, depicting different character traits in the politicians of the time. You can assess Symbolist works by Puvis de Chavannes and Moreau, and re-evaluate the official *art pompier* by artists such as Cabanel and Bouguereau, who used mythological subjects as an excuse for acres of pearly flesh. A wonderful array of Nabis works ranges from Vuillard's decorative panels of public parks to Bonnard's brilliantly simplified cat.

For a final taste of train travel, have lunch amid chandeliers and painted ceilings at the splendid restaurant (tel: 01 45 49 47 03).

Musée d'Orsay; 1 rue de la Légion d'Honneur; tel: 01 40 49 48 14; www.musee-orsay.fr; Tue–Sun 9.30am–6pm, Thur until 9.45pm; charge; map D6

Follow the banks of the Seine for books, antiques and curios

Marking the psychological and physical divide between Left Bank and Right Bank, a stroll along the River Seine provides a panorama of many of the city's greatest monuments, from the Bibliothèque de France in the east to the Eiffel Tower in the west. Plenty of stairways allow you to walk along the street-level quays or descend to the riverside banks for waterside views sprinkled with houseboats and café barges.

It's also a place of commerce and curios. Pont de Sully sees the first of the dark green boxes of the *bouquinistes*, in which the wares of second-hand book and printsellers are padlocked at night and unveiled in the afternoons in a more or less non-stop procession along the Latin Quarter and St-Germain quays (and to a lesser extent on the other side of the river, too). Some are generalists, others specialise in politics, biographies, crime novels or illustrated books, or show off old magazine covers from *L'Aurore* or *Paris Match*.

At quai Voltaire, often dubbed 'quai des Antiquaires', it's the turn of antiques shops, which occupy the fine riverside residences in a showcase that includes medieval enamels and Renaissance objets

d'art at **Brimo de Laroussilhe** (No. 7), tapestries and textiles at **Galerie Chevalier** (No. 17) and 18th-century furniture at **Anne-Marie Monin** (No. 27). A great time to visit is at the end of May, when the dealers of the Carré Rive Gauche (the square formed by quai Voltaire and rues de Beaune, de Lille and du Bac) bring out their exceptional treasures or rare discoveries.

Good places to eat along the quai des Grands-Augustins include superb Spanish restaurant **Fogon** (No. 45; tel: 01 43 54 31 33) and Guy Savoy's appropriately named, chic bistro **Les Bouquinistes** (No. 53; tel: 01 43 25 45 94). Or, join the antiques dealers at distinguished, if pricey, historic brasserie **Le Voltaire** (27 quai Voltaire; tel: 01 42 61 17 49).

Quai Voltaire; map D–E6

Feel the might of Napoleon, one-time ruler of half of Europe, and see his tomb at Les Invalides

Two immense megalomaniacs come face to face at **Les Invalides**: the Sun King Louis XIV and the Emperor Napoleon. Louis XIV built the imposing classical complex as a grandiose retirement home for soldiers wounded in his countless wars (hence the name), bringing in his finest architects Libéral Bruand and Jules Hardouin-Mansart to design the double church, vast *cour d'honneur* with its sundials and two storeys of arcades, and facades sculpted with military trophies. An equestrian relief of the king overlooks the esplanade, while Napoleon gazes down over the *cour d'honneur*.

The Eglise du Dôme – visible from all over Paris with its shiny gilding – contains the red porphyry tomb of Napoleon, transferred here in 1840 from the island of Saint Helena where he had died. In the crypt around it, relief friezes that tell of the emperor's achievements are a fascinating piece of pompous hagiography for a figure who at one point ruled half of Europe (don't expect mentions of Waterloo or Trafalgar here) and created systems of government and education still largely in place.

Much of the rest of Les Invalides is devoted to the **Musée de l'Armée**, telling the military history of France since the Middle Ages through endless galleries of armour and beautifully engraved weapons, Napoleon's frock coat and black hat (apparently he had several), to powerful film footage of the D-Day Landings. The **Historial Charles de Gaulle** is a multi-screen audiovisual presentation of the general's role in World War II and the liberation of France. More of an oddity is the **Musée des Plans-reliefs**: giant scale models of fortified French cities, originally used for planning military strategy.

Musée de l'Armée; 129 rue de Grenelle; tel: 01 44 42 38 77; www.musee-armee. fr; daily, Apr–Oct 10am–6pm, Nov–Mar 10am–5pm, closed 1st Mon of the month; charge; map C6

Count the figures on the Gates of Hell at the Musée Rodin

The newly renovated Hôtel Biron, the 18th-century mansion and spacious gardens where Rodin lived towards the end of his life, provides a beautiful setting for his work and numerous insights into what made him such a revolutionary sculptor and a bridge between the 19th-century and modern art. Different versions of *St John the Baptist* or *The Walking Man* go from realist to armless, as the artist reworked the theme. They show the incredible freedom of his approach to the body as he took inspiration from antique sculpture to cut off arms or legs, also visible in blocks of marble where portraits and nudes emerge from rough unfinished stone. Upstairs there are plaster figures and composition studies for the *Burghers of Calais,* studies for the monument to Balzac on boulevard Raspail, and paintings by Van Gogh, Renoir and some of the other artists collected by Rodin.

One room is devoted to the tormented sculptures of Camille Claudel, Rodin's young pupil and mistress, including the extraordinary *The Wave* with bronze figures of bathers dwarfed by a giant green marble wave.

After visiting the house, the towering bronze *The Gates of Hell,* outside, now appears rather like a summary of Rodin's art, swarming with small versions of many of the sculptures visible in the house – including *Three Shades, Ugolino,* and the famous *The Thinker*.

Many more sculptures are dotted around the gardens, while temporary exhibitions are put on in the restored chapel. The museum has a popular, relaxed outdoor café, or if you're feeling flush you might like to try **Arpège** (84 rue de Varenne; tel: 01 47 05 09 06; www.alain-passard. com), where Alain Passard's vegetarian haute cuisine has earned him three Michelin stars.

Musée Rodin; 77 rue de Varenne; tel: 01 44 18 61 10; www.musee-rodin.fr; Tue–Sun 10am–5.45pm; charge; map C6

Get right down under the belly of the Iron Lady for the most spine-tingling views

Among nicknames for the **Eiffel Tower** are *la dame de fer* (the iron lady) and *la grande oreille* (the big ear), the latter relating to the use of its radio station to listen in on enemy messages during World War I. Intended to show off France's engineering prowess for the World Fair of 1889, on the centenary of the French Revolution, the tower was significantly constructed on the Champ de Mars, the former military parade ground where celebrations for the anniversary of the Revolution were held in the 1790s. At 300 metres/984ft (today, 324 metres/1,063ft with radio aerials) it was the tallest building in the world. As with many modern arrivals, Gustave Eiffel's structure was initially feared or detested by many. During its construction, Garnier, Dumas fils and Maupassant were among those who signed a petition against it, poet François Coppée wrote 'the monster is hideous', 'an ugly colossus' and 'a Yankee dream', while William Morris claimed to go up it every day for lunch simply to avoid having to see it from afar. But Gustave Eiffel defended his project: 'I believe, for my part, that the tower will have its own beauty.' In the end it was completed in just two years, two months and five days, and opinions soon changed. The fascinating structure drew nearly two million visitors during the world fair and now regularly receives 7 million visitors a year.

The tower was intended to be temporary, but was saved by its role in telecommunications: France's first wireless transmission was made from here to the Panthéon in 1898, from 1903 it was used for military transmissions, and during World War I, the big ear intercepted crucial messages during the Battle of the Marne. It is still used for radio broadcasts and, since 2005, for TNT.

Naturally, most people climb to the top for the views over Paris; but the really exciting views to be had are those of the Iron Lady herself. The metal structure looks impressive as you walk underneath its four legs or as you rise up in the vintage double-decker lifts, passing a constantly changing spider's web of metal girders and the 2.5 million rivets that hold them together. Two stops punctuate the way up. The first level has the **58 Eiffel brasserie** (located 58 metres/190ft above ground level), souvenir shops and an ice rink at Christmas. A recent renovation has installed a breath-taking glass floor and a multi-media 'cultural path' featuring little-known information about the tower. Gourmet restaurant **Jules Verne** (tel: 01 45 55 61 44) is on the second level at 115 metres/377ft (reached by its own lift). The third level at 275 metres/984ft brings you to Gustave Eiffel's cosy office, a champagne bar and a viewing deck. The tower spar-kles nightly with thousands of tiny lights, on the hour from nightfall until 1am.

You can book in advance online. However, should you arrive ticket-less, queues are usually shorter on foggy days or late at night.

Eiffel Tower; Champ de Mars; tel: 08 92 70 12 39; www.tour-eiffel.fr; mid-June–Aug daily 9am–12.45am, last lift to top 11pm, Sept–mid-June daily 9.30am–11.45pm, last lift to top 10.30pm; charge; map A6

Pose for sculptor Maillol on rue de Grenelle, where the Musée Maillol occupies a lovely mansion

In the early 18th century when the Marais had gone out of fashion, nobles and civil servants jostled to put up mansions just outside the city walls in the Faubourg St-Germain. Streets like rue de Grenelle, rue de Varenne and rue Vaneau are still lined with these residences, many of them now embassies and government ministries. The **Musée Maillol** is a rare one that can be visited, with Aristide Maillol's sculptures, modern art and excellent temporary exhibitions displayed around the panelled rooms of the beautiful Hôtel Bouchardon.

The museum was created in 1995 by Dina Vierny as a tribute to Maillol, but it also tells you a lot about diminutive, Romanian-born Vierny, who first posed for the elderly sculptor in 1934 when aged only 15. She was the model for some of his most celebrated sculptures, such as *Spring*, *Air* and *Harmony*, proving the perfect beauty for his idealised classical forms. She also sat for other artists including Matisse and Dufy. Later, as a collector and gallerist, she gathered drawings by Matisse and Picasso, Surrealist objects by Marcel Duchamp and championed Russian artists and naive painters.

The museum covers all stages of Maillol's career, including tapestries, ceramics and little-known early paintings and pastels when he was associated with the Nabis.

The museum has a pleasant Italian café in the cellar. In the street outside is the splendid *Fountain of the Four Seasons*, sculpted by Edmé Bouchardon in 1739–45, with allegorical figures representing the city of Paris.

Musée Maillol; 61 rue de Grenelle; tel: 01 42 22 59 58; www.museemaillol.com; check website for opening times; charge; map D5

Explore non-Western cultures at the Musée du Quai Branly

An enormous success since it opened in 2005, the **Musée du Quai Branly** is the culmination of former President Chirac's pet project to create a showcase for art from non-Western cultures; for which Jean Nouvel's long colourful building, perched on stilts in an increasingly jungle-like wild garden created by Gilles Clément, provides a baroque and other-worldly environment. Inside, a large ramp curves up to the permanent collection, which is arranged in four zones: Asia, Africa, the Americas and Oceania. Although colour-coded by continent, it is also intended to span cultures and allow you to wander from one to the other.

The displays go beyond the usual preconceptions of tribal art with an incredible variety of items, from Gabonese masks, North American Indian painted cowhides and astonishing carved beams and lintels from Papua New Guinea, to modern Aboriginal paintings – with photographs, film footage and sound recordings enhancing the experience. The emphasis is on theatricality and aura rather than a dry academic take. Many cases are dimly lit, partly for conservation reasons, partly to create a sense of magic. Some items, such as the fragile Ethiopian religious paintings, are displayed shrine-like in the 27 boxes that protrude from the building's facade.

A huge collection of musical instruments is stored in view in a large glass core that rises up through the building, fitting in with the transversal approach. As well as the exhibitions programme, concerts, theatre and dance are performed in either the auditorium or outdoor amphitheatre.

Musée du Quai Branly; 37 quai Branly; tel: 01 56 61 70 00; www.quaibranly.fr; Tue, Wed, Sun 11am–7pm, Thur–Sat 11am–9pm; charge; map A7

Dream about cake at the Pâtisserie des Rêves and Hugo & Victor

Let them eat cake (or rather, brioche), Marie-Antoinette supposedly tactlessly remarked on the fate of the hungry populace, but who would have thought that designer cakes would became the showground for 21st-century creativity? 'Designer' in the literal sense: today's top pastry chefs sketch out their ideas, produce seasonal collections and present them. Cakes are indeed the stuff of dreams at the **Pâtisserie des Rêves** (pictured), where Philippe Conticini's creations are displayed like jewels under a pyramid of gleaming glass cloches. Gems include a Saint-Honoré with caramel and an artistic wave of cream, a chocolate éclair that sits within a tube of chocolate and a flower-shaped Paris-Brest. Around the corner at **Hugo & Victor**, inspiration comes in a more literary form, with a black glass and chrome interior and chocolate boxes that look like books. Pastry chef Hugues Pouget works with eight key flavours: chocolate, vanilla and caramel year round along with five changing, seasonal flavours. Each features in glossy marble-like chocolates and two gâteaux – experimental Hugo and more classic Victor – along with a wine suggestion to match each flavour group.

Want to make your cake part of a chic picnic? **La Grande Epicerie**, the food hall of Le Bon Marché department store, is a favourite with ladies who shop, particularly noted for its Italian deli counter.

Pâtisserie des Rêves; 93 rue du Bac; tel: 01 42 84 00 82; www.lapatisseriedesreves. com; Tue–Sat 9am–8pm, Sun 9am–6pm; map D5
Hugo & Victor; 40 Boulevard Raspail; tel: 01 44 39 97 73; www.hugovictor.com; Mon–Fri and Sun 10am–7pm, Sat 9am–8pm; map D5
La Grande Epicerie; 38 rue de Sèvres; tel: 01 44 39 81 00; www.lagrandeepicerie. com; Mon–Sat 8.30am–9pm; map D5

Feast with the foodies on rue St-Dominique

In the Paris of embassies, ministries and old money, smart residents and civil servants like to eat well, and rue St-Dominique could almost be renamed Christian Constant Street. After being chef at Le Crillon, Constant opened elegant bistro **Le Violon d'Ingres** (No. 135; tel: 01 45 55 15 05). Since then he has added **Café Constant** (No. 139), an all-day, no-reservation, café-bistro, where you can come to read the paper over coffee or a meal; and **Les Cocottes** (No. 135), his stylish take on a casual diner where the concept is grandmotherly home cooking, slow-baked in *cocottes* (cast-iron casserole dishes).

A little further on, overlooking a fountain on a small arcaded square, **La Fontaine de Mars** (No. 129; tel: 01 47 05 46 44) is all red and white check tablecloths and old apéritif posters. Renowned for its traditional southwestern specialities, it was propelled into the spotlight when Barrack Obama dined here with his family.

Downstairs at **Hôtel Thoumieux** (No. 79; tel: 01 47 05 79 00; www.thoumieux.fr) is a classy vintage brasserie, while upstairs, in gourmet **Restaurant Sylvestre**, with just 20 seats in a neo-1950s decor

that smacks of being invited round to someone's apartment, Franco-Pakistani chef Sylvestre Wahid serves up his technically accomplished dishes – usually with a hint of spice. Around the corner, **L'Ami Jean** (27 rue Malar; tel: 01 47 05 86 89) is a leader of the *bistronomique* trend – read gastronomic food in a bistro atmosphere at economical prices – a raucous Basque tavern setting for Stéphane Jego's generous, lovely dishes served to a clientele of rugby fans and foodies.

Rue St-Dominique; map B6

Relive artistic Montparnasse through its classic brasseries

Montparnasse's artistic and intellectual heyday can almost be spelled out by the string of brasseries along its boulevard, once a home from home to a roll call of artists and writers who epitomised the dynamic age of modern art, jazz and cocktails, and the international melting-pot of the Ecole de Paris – Italian Modigliani, later the Surrealists Picasso and Cocteau, American photographer Man Ray. Modern development has taken its toll on the boulevard, but there's still some wonderful people-watching of oyster eaters and cinema goers to be had.

When **La Coupole** (118 boulevard du Montparnasse; tel: 01 43 20 14 20; pictured) opened in 1927, it was the city's largest restaurant, with columns painted by different artists, Art Deco lights and mosaics, and basement 'dansing' where couples danced the sexy new tango imported from Argentina. You can sit in the window for a drink or inside at white-napped tables for oysters, shellfish, or its unexpected house speciality of lamb curry. **Le Select** (No. 99; tel: 01 45 48 38 14), across the street, still has the aura of a speakeasy and a sign proclaiming 'bar américain'; **La Rotonde** (No. 105; tel: 01 43 26 48 26), opened in 1911, is a cocoon of brass and red velvet; and **Le Dôme** (No. 108; tel: 01 43 35 25 81) has become a luxury fish restaurant. But something of the old spirit survives at **Le Rosebud** (11 bis rue Delambre; tel: 01 43 35 38 54), a cocktail bar that never quite fades from fashion. Further along the boulevard, **La Closerie des Lilas** (No. 171; tel: 01 40 51 34 50) is still favoured by writers and politicians. Get in the mood over a cocktail in the piano bar, as you sit at a table where a brass plaque might just indicate that Hemingway, Trotsky or Picasso sat there before you.

Boulevard du Montparnasse; map D-E3

Descend 130 steps under Paris to its skeletal foundations: the macabre world of the Catacombes

'Stop, this is the Empire of death!' sets the tone for the philosophical musings that accompany you around the **Catacombes de Paris**, reached after a descent down 130 steps and a walk along a tunnel that takes you through a section of the labyrinth of quarries dug out since Roman times – like a veritable gruyère cheese under the city – passing on the way an extraordinary sculpture of Fort Mahon in Majorca.

The Catacombes, or 'municipal ossuary', was created in the late 18th century when the city's overcrowded, malodorous and unhygienic cemeteries were cleared out and, between 1786 and 1860, the bones of some six million Parisians transferred here. But it was in 1810 that Louis-Etienne Héricart de Thury, inspector general of the quarries, had the idea of putting the bones in neat formations, arranging them in the incredibly neat piles of long bones with bands of skulls, sometimes in great circular sweeps, that make the Catacombes a setting for reflecting on death, memory and the fragility of human life. Plaques listing the cemetery the remains were taken from and the date, along with macabre quotations by writers and philosophers such as Lamartine and Molière, complete the picture.

The Catacombes were opened to visitors almost as soon as they were created and, as well as some illustrious official visitors, Napoleon III included, have ever since also attracted urban myths and illicit party-goers (often not in the catacombs themselves but in the parts of other quarries located around the city).

Bring a jumper if you visit in summer – the quarries are a chilly 14°C all year round.

Les Catacombes de Paris; 1 avenue du Colonel Rol-Tanguy, place Denfert-Rochereau; tel: 01 43 22 47 63; www.catacombes.paris.fr; Tue–Sun 10am–8pm, last entrance 7pm; charge; map E1

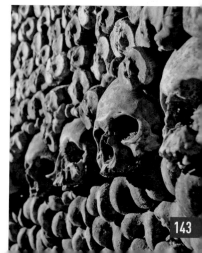

Dredge under the capital for an insight into its inner workings: the labyrinthine Paris sewers

A walk around the **Egouts de Paris** is probably the only chance most of us will ever have of visiting a sewer – an educational insight into the underground workings of a great city and the ebb and flow of its water and effluents. Although it's often billed as a children's attraction, it's more of a sub-urban trip around the entrails of the city, testimony to the less visible engineering prowess behind the capital's 19th-century expansion. Blue enamel signs announcing avenue Bosquet or rue Cognacq-Jay mirror those labelling the streets up above so that sewer workers can know exactly where they are. The tour takes in just a tiny propor-

tion of the 2,400km (1,490 miles) of dank galleries under the capital, as you walk past canals and channels, sluices and pumps, accompanied by the constant sound of rushing water, and an array of dredging barges and machines to keep everything flowing. Panels describe the history of the sewers, from the very first covered sewer (before which there were only open drains) on rue Montmartre in 1370, during the reign of Charles V. In the 1850s, Baron Haussmann's chief engineer, Eugène Belgrand, masterminded the creation of today's sewage and water distribution system, a system not just about sewage but also about providing drinking water to Parisians, drainage and the control of flood water. It involved a sewer in every street, forming a complex web as small sewers flowed into successively larger channels, and a double water supply system, providing drinking water for homes and non-drinking water to clean the streets.

Egouts de Paris; Pont de l'Alma, Left Bank, facing 93 quai d'Orsay; tel: 01 53 68 27 81; www.paris.fr; May–Sept Sat–Wed 11am–5pm, Oct–Apr Sat–Wed 11am–4pm, closed 25 Dec–1 Jan and 2 weeks in Jan; charge; map B7

Be a fly on the wall in an early 20th-century artist's studio in Montparnasse

Today Antoine Bourdelle is chiefly remembered as a creator of muscular Modernist sculptures and, in an obscure art historical link, as assistant of Rodin and teacher of Giacometti. However, the small **Musée Bourdelle**, centred around Bourdelle's old studio and family apartment, also offers a vision of artists' Montparnasse at the start of the 20th century. Several large works, including figures for Bourdelle's equestrian monument to Argentine general Alvéar, are displayed in the garden and a 1960s extension; while a new wing contains some of the countless busts of Beethoven through which, like Rodin with Balzac, Bourdelle explored tortured, creative genius and endlessly worked through different moods and character traits. But the most atmospheric part of the museum is the overgrown row of dusty artists' studios, where Bourdelle had his atelier from 1885 until his death in 1929. Happily, it hasn't been too tidied up.

Musée Bourdelle, 18 rue Antoine-Bourdelle; tel: 01 49 54 73 73; www.bourdelle.paris.fr, Tue–Sun 10am–6pm; free, charge during exhibitions; map C3

Montparnasse artists' trail

Villa Vassilieff (21 avenue du Maine; tel: 01 43 25 88 32; www.villa vassilieff.net). The atelier where Russian artist Marie Vassilieff ran an art academy and canteen and threw exotic parties.

Musée Zadkine (100 bis rue d'Assas; tel: 01 43 26 91 90; www.zadkine. paris.fr). The house and studio of the Russian-born sculptor and wife Valentine Prax.

Fondation Henri Cartier-Bresson (2 impasse Lebouis; tel: 01 56 80 27 00; www.henricartierbresson. org). The studio house now contains Cartier-Bresson's archives and presents shows of his work and other photographers.

BEYOND THE CENTRE

Beyond the Centre

GENNEVILLIERS

BOIS-
COLOMBES

ASNIÈRES-
SUR-SEINE

Île des
Vannes

Cimetière des
Chiens

SAINT-OUEN

LA GARENNE-
COLOMBES

PORT DE CLICHY

CLICHY

Puces de
St-Ouen

COURBEVOIE

Île de
Grande Jatte

LEVALLOIS-
PERRET

EPINETTES

18

NANTERRE

LA
DÉFENSE

PUTEAUX

NEUILLY-
SUR-SEINE

TERNES

MONTMARTE

Île de
Puteaux

JARDIN
D'ACLIMATATION

Fondation
Louis Vuitton

Arc de
Triomphe

Gare
St-Lazare

SURESNES

Lac
Inférieur

CHAILLOT

Grand
Palais

Petit
Palais

Musée du
Louvre

BOIS DE
BOULOGNE

Musée Marmottan Monet
La Gare

Tour Eiffel

Musée
d'Orsay

Hippodrome
de Longchamp

Hippodrome
d'Auteuil

Fondation
Hippocrène

Fondation
Le Corbusier

Hôtel des
Invalides

AUTEUIL

GRENELLE

Palais du
Luxembourg

Panthéo

Tour
Montparnasse

Gare
Montparnasse

BOULOGNE-
BILLANCOURT

PARC
GEORGES
BRASSENS

14

DOMAINE
NATIONAL DE
ST-CLOUD

SÈVRES

Musée National
de la Céramique

ISSY-LES-
MOULINEAUX

VANVES

PARC
MONTSOURS

Île Seguin

Île
St-Germain

MALAKOFF

MONTROUGE

Orly

Marvel at the world's largest collection of Monets then check out Paris's latest contemporary art centre

Poised in upmarket residential Paris, the **Musée Marmottan Monet** (pictured) is a dignified Second Empire villa where you just happen to find the largest collection of works by Claude Monet in the world. Many of them were bequeathed by Monet's son Michel, and you can follow all the stages of the artist's œuvre including *Impression, Soleil Levant* – the pink-skied view of the port at Le Havre that gave its name to the Impressionist movement – rare caricatures, early landscapes and portraits of his children, sketchbooks and the artist's palette too. The holy of holies is the circular basement room hung with a series of vibrantly coloured paintings of Monet's water garden at Giverny (see also Musée de l'Orangerie, page 55). Monet created the garden with an eye to painting it, as a growing artwork in its own right, selecting plants and creating viewpoints and patches of light and shadow. And here, amid the rich blues and viridian green, are glimpses and reflections of water lilies, weeping willows, the Japanese bridge and the punt moored to the bank. The museum also has other fine Impressionist works by Caillebotte, Sisley, Manet and Pissarro, and several of Berthe Morisot's tender paintings of children.

While you're in the Bois de Boulogne area, be sure to check out the new Frank Gehry-designed **Fondation Louis Vuitton**. This futuristic, ship-like structure is home to the foundation's contemporary art collection and cultural centre, complete with art bookshop and gourmet restaurant.

Musée Marmottan Monet, 2 rue Louis-Boilly; tel: 01 44 96 50 33; www.marmottan. fr;Tue–Sun 10am–6pm, Thur until 9pm; charge; map B2
Fondation Louis Vuitton, 8 avenue du Mahatma Gandhi; tel: 01 40 69 96 00; www.fondationlouisvuitton.fr; Mon, Wed–Fri noon–7pm, until 11pm Fri, Sat-Sun 11am–8pm; charge; map B3

Stand in the home of Modernity: avant-garde icons by Le Corbusier in Auteuil

If you're interested in modern architecture, then adjoining Villas La Roche and Jeanneret (now **Fondation Le Corbusier**), built 1923–25, are fascinating. Here, in the small but clever building full of light and interesting views, you can see Le Corbusier putting his ideas into practice early in his career, using reinforced concrete in what would become his celebrated five principles of architecture: pilottis, strip windows, open-plan spaces, roof terraces and ingenious built-in furniture, intended to meet all the needs of modern living. This is no modern white box. If the outside is all crisp and white, inside the architect experimented with colours on certain walls to alter the perception of volumes.

For all its staid image today, plush Auteuil boasted plenty of adventurous patrons in the 1920s. One street away, almost all of rue

Mallet-Stevens was designed by Robert Mallet-Stevens, the elegant dandy of the Modern Movement. His own architectural offices now belong to the **Fondation Hippocrène**, which supports European artists and writers and is open for exhibitions and events – a chance to admire its Cubist volumes and characteristic use of iron and glass.

More Le Corbusier in Paris

Other Paris buildings by the architect include the Molitor apartment block, where you can visit Le Corbusier's apartment and architectural studio (24 rue Nungessor et Coli; tel: 01 42 88 75 72, by appointment); and two blocks at the Cité Universitaire (17 boulevard Jourdain) and the Armée du Salut hostel (rue Cantagrel).

Fondation Le Corbusier, 10 square du Dr Blanche; tel: 01 42 88 75 72; www.fondationlecorbusier.fr; Mon 1.30–6pm, Tue–Sat 10–6pm, tours in English Tue 2pm; charge; map B2 Fondation Hippocrène, 12 rue Mallet-Stevens; tel 01 45 20 95 94; www.fondation-hippocrene.fr; during exhibitions Tue–Sat 2–7pm; map B2

Get on the nature trail along La Petite Ceinture, a green belt along the tracks of a disused railway

Unlike the manicured look of Parisian parks, **La Petite Ceinture** nature trail between Gare d'Auteuil and La Muette (rue de Ranelagh) is a cheerfully overgrown tangle of grass and bushes, a wonderful vision of the town reconquered by nature on the embankments and former tracks of the Petite Ceinture (little belt) railway that once encircled Paris. Panels point out the different habitats – meadow, woodland, scrub with bushes, clematis and honeysuckle, wetland with willows, limestone spur and the cutting wall colonised by ferns and creepers – surrounded only by birdsong from tits, warblers and woodpeckers. At the end of the promenade, the red brick Passy-La Muette station has been converted into **La Gare** (19 chaussée de la Muette; tel: 01 42 15 15 31; www. restaurantlagare.com), a stylish restaurant with tables spread out along the platforms, and a bar set in the former ticket office.

The 32km (20-mile) – long railway was built between 1852 and 1869 to connect the different main lines, first to carry goods, later transporting Parisians as a forerunner of the Métro. The line closed to passenger trains in 1934 (it continued for freight until 1993), but still fascinates, with fans who campaign for its preservation. You can glimpse traces of it all over town: cuttings as you walk in Parc Montsouris and Parc des Buttes-Chaumont, a tunnel under Parc Georges Brassens, lone railway bridges or remaining stations such as the Gare de Charonne, now the Flèche d'Or (see page 156).

Another short section has been turned into a nature trail and community garden in the 12th *arrondissement*, reached from square Charles Péguy, where it joins the **Promenade Plantée** (along the disused Bastille–Vincennes line); and a new footpath will follow in the 15th *arrondissement*, bringing a touch of wilderness between rue St-Charles and rue Olivier de Serres.

La Petite Ceinture nature trail; map B2 and E–F2

Attend an open studio or shop for organic goodies at municipal undertaker's turned art space the 104

The echoing halls of the **CentQuatre** (104) resound to dance steps and video installations – not bad for a place that used to be the municipal undertaker's. In its time, the vast neoclassical building contained stabling for 2,000 horses, storerooms and workshops for making coffins and hearses. After closing in 1998, it was refurbished as a complex of artists' studios, rehearsal rooms and performance spaces set around a glazed central hall conceived as an internal street – open, if windswept, to visitors and local inhabitants.

The approach is multi-disciplinary so that at any one time residents might include artists, musicians, theatre directors, choreographers, DJs or landscape designers. All open their studios to the public on a regular basis, although, as this is considered a place for creation rather than presentation, there may not be much to see when you visit. A programme of exhibitions, concerts and performances, children's workshops in La Maison des Petits (Little People's House) and urban dance sessions offer other alternatives. Old-fashioned guinguette dances, vinyl-listening sessions and stretching classes are also on the menu. **Grand Central**, a funky industrial loft-style brasserie is a popular weekend brunch spot, while the **Emmaüs Défi** charity shop (Wed–Sat) breathes new life into furniture and objects, a business incubator is being set up, and there's an organic food market on Saturdays. After a slow start, the CentQuatre is definitely finding its place in the Paris cultural scene.

Le CentQuatre; 5 rue Curial or 104 rue d'Aubervilliers; tel: 01 54 35 50 00; www.104.fr; Tue–Fri noon–7pm, Sat–Sun 11am–7pm; closed 2 weeks in Aug; exhibitions free, performances charge; map E4

153

Learn about satellites at La Villette: a day at the Cité des Sciences, Philharmonie 2 and modern park

With the Cité des Sciences on one side, Cité de la Musique (now Philharmonie 2)on the other and the Parc de la Villette stretching between the two, **La Villette** was part of a vast transformation project started in the 1980s to revive this corner of northwest Paris, site of the old abattoirs and livestock market. As urban renewal, it's done pretty well. You can see films in the spherical mirrored **Géode** IMAX cinema (pictured), go round the **Argonaute**, a 1950s submarine, follow an undulating path along the Canal de l'Ourcq, which cuts through the centre of the park, explore themed gardens, and go to rock concerts or jazz festivals.

The **Cité des Sciences et de l'Industrie**, a hi-tech science museum, has all the expected hands-on explanations of sound, light, images and mathematics, while other sections look more at technology's effect on modern life, with energy and transport examined for instance. When it comes to satellites, the idea is not so much us looking up at space but how satellites look down on us, surveying both where we are and the state of the planet.

Outside, 26 red metal structures or '*folies*', designed by Swiss architect Bernard Tschumi, dot the park like points on a grid, serving various functions including burger bar, in-

formation kiosk, bandstand and first aid post. Across the Canal St-Martin, a serpentine path leads through a trail of themed gardens designed by artists and architects, with bamboo plants and Buren's pebble stripes, Fabrice Hyber's anti-memorial for Aids, vines and fountains, spooky noises, and a dune garden with trampolines and pedal windmills for small children.

Perhaps the best time of all to appreciate the park is during the **Cinéma en Plein Air** (mid-July–mid-Aug) outdoor film festival, when you can relax on the lawn and watch great movies projected on a giant screen at nightfall.

A few relics of the old livestock market remain: the **Grande Halle**, the **Théâtre Paris-Villette** and the former vets' pavilion now restored as the **WIP Villette**, dedicated to hip hop and street art. Next to the Grande Halle is Jean Nouvel's new €390 million **Philharmonie de Paris**, or **Philharmonie 1**, home to the Orchestre de Paris and a 2,400-seat symphonic concert hall, and the former **Cité de la Musique**, now known as **Philharmonie 2**, which houses a spectacular music museum. Around 1,000 musical instruments, including Chopin's Pleyel grand piano, Stradivarius violins,

beautiful harpsichords, serpents, synthesizers and Algerian lutes are displayed amid paintings and sculpture to put them in context, and you might come across mini recitals as you walk around. This is one place where the audio guide truly makes a difference, playing the sound of some of the instruments on display and extracts of music ranging from Scarlatti, Offenbach and Dowland to a Hammond organ. The concert hall is a clever, modulable space putting on an incredibly broad range of music, from early music and symphonies to jazz and world music.

There are cafés and places to eat around the park, but for a taste of the old meat traders' Villette, indulge in a humongous steak at **Au Bœuf Couronné** (188 avenue Jean-Jaurès; tel: 01 42 39 44 44), a survivor of the market brasseries opposite the park.

Philharmonie de Paris; 221 avenue Jean-Jaurès; tel: 01 44 84 44 84; www.philharmoniedeparis.fr; Tue–Fri noon–6pm, Sat–Sun 10am–6pm, concert times vary; charge; map F4
Cité des Sciences et de l'Industrie; 30 avenue Corentin-Cariou; tel: 01 40 05 80 00; www.cite-sciences.fr; Tue–Sat 10am–6pm, Sun 10am–7pm; charge; map F4
Parc de la Villette; www.villette.com; daily 24 hours; free; map F4

Chill out in villagey Charonne

Northeast Paris gives a taste of the old working-class Paris, offering a sometimes slightly schizoid mix of picturesque villagey remnants and 1970s tower-block horrors.

The square-towered **Eglise St-Germain-de-Charonne**, dating from the 12th to the 15th centuries, still forms the heart of old village Charonne, with its cemetery climbing up the hill behind it. Opposite the church, pedestrianised rue St-Blaise, once the village high street, has a bucolic air, with its ateliers and bistros – try **Café Lumière** (No. 15; tel: 09 50 58 76 86) for a meal – and little gardens. Prettily renovated Square des Grès, once the site of a pillory, stands as an unlikely crossroads between gentrification and a vast public housing estate.

Trendy hotel/restaurant **Mama**

Shelter (109 rue de Bagnolet; tel: 01 43 48 48 48; www.mamashelter. com), designed by Philippe Starck, confirms the area's ascent in fashion terms, with a concrete-chic restaurant, cocktail bar and DJs at weekends, as well as outdoor tables overlooking the Petite Ceinture (see page 152). Charonne's former train station is now the **Flèche d'Or** (No. 102 bis; tel: 01 44 64 01 02; www. flechedor.fr) music venue.

In a small park up the street is the **Pavillon de l'Ermitage** (148 rue de Bagnolet; tel: 01 40 24 15 95; www.pavillondelermitage.com; Mar–July, Sept–mid-Dec Thu–Sun 2–5.30pm; charge), a rococo summer house built for 'Madame', the daughter of Louis XIV and Madame de Montespan, in the grounds of the long-gone Domaine de Bagnolet back when the gentry had their country retreats in the area.

Minutes away is what estate agents today refer to as 'the countryside comes to Paris': the streets of tightly packed, creeper-covered houses and stairways around rue Mondonville, rue Jules-Siegfried and rue Irénée-Blanc, built for the labourers at the local gypsum quarries of yore.

Charonne; map F2

Discover global Paris at the Cité de l'Immigration

By an ironic twist of history, the Palais de la Porte Dorée constructed for the 1931 Colonial Exhibition, has become a centre recounting the history of two centuries of immigration to France. Documents, artefacts, archive photos, artworks and sound recordings explore the breadth of the subject. Immigration has not just been from the former colonies in West and North Africa and from Southeast Asia, but has also seen Polish miners come to the north of France, Italian labourers, Eastern European Jews prior to World War II, white Russians and refugees from the Spanish Civil War. What brings these histories alive are the individual stories, told via personal recordings or through the donated items particularly significant of past and new lives: photos, a school certificate, battered suitcases, a sewing machine. Some striking modern art includes Barthélémy Toguo's witty six-high stack of bunk beds, weighed under by the characteristic checked carrier bags of immigrants in an over-crowded migrant workers' hostel.

The building is a fabulous piece of 1930s architecture, with a sweeping colonnaded facade covered with reliefs of pith-hatted hunters, jungle beasts and palm trees, and redolent of colonialism, a frescoed Salle des Fêtes, and two superb Art Deco offices still with their original zebra wood furniture designed by Eugène Printz and Emile-Jacques Ruhlmann. The basement contains another relic of 1931 – the enormously popular aquarium, originally intended to introduce the French public to the marine life of its colonies. It is always awash with colourful fish and children, watching to see if the inhabitants of the crocodile pit will pounce. The last of the Nile crocodiles brought here in 1948 died in 2009 and were replaced by four Mississippi alligators.

Cité de l'Immigration; 293 avenue Daumesnil; tel: 01 53 59 58 60; www. histoire-immigration.fr; www.aquarium-portedoree.fr; Tue–Fri 10am–5.30pm, Sat, Sun 10am–7pm; charge; map F1

Bring gifts to Buddha in the 13th arrondissement, Chinatown

The tower blocks of the 13th *arrondissement* don't look too prepossessing at first glance, but Paris's largest Chinatown, concentrated along avenue d'Ivry and avenue de Choisy, has an identity all its own, with the crowds and businesses giving it an invigorating feel of Hong Kong.

Life centres around the two enormous supermarkets, **Tang Frères** (48 avenue d'Ivry) and **Paris Store** (44 avenue d'Ivry), filled with mangosteens and dragon fruit, noodles and wonton wrappers, obscure sweets and jellies, not to mention departments devoted to cooking pots, porcelain and plastic flowers. Above the street, on the esplanade of the **Olympiades** shopping centre, a line of pagoda-shaped pavilions

is apparently a happy coincidence – built to attract middle-class residents but colonised instead by Asian immigrants and now containing Asian restaurants. Many of the restaurants here are pan-Asian, serving a mixture of Chinese, Vietnamese, Laotian and Thai dishes. Go to **Pho 14** (129 avenue de Choisy; tel: 01 45 83 61 15) for an authentic formica-style Vietnamese eatery, always busy with diners slurping *pho* soup – a broth thick with rice noodles and topped with pork, meatballs or slices of beef, into which you add beansprouts and mint leaves. **Lao Lane Xang 2** (102 avenue d'Ivry; tel: 01 58 89 00 00) is known for its Laotian and Thai dishes with a simpler sibling establishment across the street at No. 105.

There is more to Chinatown than slurping noodles however. Off avenue d'Ivry, just as rue du Disque appears to descend into an underground car park, a few steps bring you to the **Autel du Culte Bouddhiste**, where amid dangling red lanterns and the smell of incense, people place offerings of fruit, rice or cooking oil before small altars – it's like you've really been transported to Asia.

Chinatown; map E1

Go on a treasure hunt at the Puces de St-Ouen, Paris's biggest flea market

Described as the largest antiques market in the world, the location of the **Puces de St-Ouen** harks back to the days when rag-and-bone men were allowed to sell goods, free of duty, just outside the city walls. Today it has been listed for its unique style and character, a lure for thousands of visitors each weekend. However, to describe the Puces de St-Ouen as a market hardly gives you an idea of its scale: over 2,500 individual dealers spread across more than a dozen markets, most of them strung along the rue des Rosiers. There's everything, from classy antiques to incredible junk, and an ever-growing fashion for modern design and collectables.

Marché Vernaison is atmospheric and eclectic, the oldest and most flea of the markets, encompassing 300 stalls in a triangle of alleys. Hidden in its depths, touristy but fun *bistro-chansonnier* **Chez Louisette** serves mussels and chips while singers belt out Piaf. Nearby **Marché Biron** is mainly devoted to period antiques for those with a taste for ormolu and chandeliers.

Marché Dauphine, purpose-built in the 1990s, has plenty of high-quality goods, with antique mirrors and barometers at Leda, 19th-century aperitif sets, carpets, paintings, toys and watches. Take an escalator to the first floor for vintage clothes, books and postcards. **Marché Serpette** is indoors and rather chic, where you might find historic panelling, Art Deco furniture and wonderful costume jewellery at Olwen Forest. Stallholders set out tables for lunch and play chess between visitors. **Marché Paul Bert**, which runs round the sides, is a decorators' favourite, with eclectic furniture, garden statuary, great kitchenwares specialist Bachelier and lots of 20th-century design.

There are plenty of bars and bistros, and should your purchase be too big to get into a suitcase, transporter and shipping company representatives are on the spot.

Puces de St-Ouen, St-Ouen; Sat–Mon 8am–6pm; map D4

159

Pay homage to man's best friend – and Kiki the monkey – at the Cimetière des Chiens

Bordering the Seine at Asnières-sur-Seine, the dog cemetery is a moving shrine to much-loved pets. The oldest pet cemetery in the world was opened in 1899 by militant feminist journalist Marguerite Durand and lawyer Georges Harmois, who bought the site on the Ile des Ravageurs (now no longer quite an island as the channel has been filled in). Architect Eugène Petit designed a grandiose entrance in a mix of Art Nouveau and Moorish styles, gateway to the gravestones not just of dogs but lots of cats, a racehorse or two, Kiki the monkey, Cocotte the hen and assorted budgerigars and hamsters.

Facing the entrance is a grand monument to Barry, the Saint Bernard, with a sculpture of a small child riding on the back of a mountain rescue dog: 'He saved the life of 40 people. He was killed by the 41st'. Then there are a few stars such as Rin Tin Tin, the Alsatian who starred in numerous Hollywood films in the 1920s and 30s, an endless cast of Mimis and Mitzis, Rexes, Pompons, Loulous, Betsys and Oscars, and a living population of stray cats sleeping on the gravestones.

It helps if you can read a little French to make the most of the moving epitaphs, messages to faithful companions and tales of lonely lives – 'Disappointed by humans, never by my dog' is one. And amidst it all, there are perhaps a few happy endings too, as in: 'On the 15th May 1958 was buried here the errant dog who died at the gates of the cemetery and was the 40,000th beast to find eternal rest in Asnières dog cemetery.'

Cimetière des Chiens; 4 Pont de Clichy, Asnières-sur-Seine; tel: 01 40 86 21 11; www.asnieres-sur-seine.fr; Tue–Sun 10am–6pm, winter until 4.30pm; charge; map C4

Frequent the royals at the Basilique St-Denis

One thousand years ago, the sub-urb of St-Denis, north of Paris, had a very different image to the one it has today. Then it was considered a sacred spot, a place of pilgrimage ever since early Christian martyr Denis had ended up here – carrying his head, which had been chopped off in Montmartre. Today, the magnificent Gothic **basilica** comes as a surprise amid the modern multicultural suburb, home to the remains of docks and premises from its Industrial Age heyday.

Begun in the 12th century over an earlier church, the basilica is considered the first true Gothic structure with its ogival vaulting and rose window. It is particularly lovely for classical concerts every June during the Festival St-Denis but, above all, it is fascinating as the burial place of French monar-chy. In the crypt are traces of the Carolingian church and a 12th-century crypt, where the remains of Louis XVI, Marie Antoinette and the last of the Bourbons are buried.

St-Denis's other landmark is the **Stade de France**, constructed just in time for France's victory in the 1998 World Cup, and instantly recognisable with its flying-saucer roof. You can tour the stadium, visiting the stands and changing rooms and running out onto the pitch through the players' tunnel.

Basilique St-Denis; 1 rue de la Légion d'Honneur; tel: 01 48 09 83 54; www.saint-denis.monuments-nationaux.fr; Mon–Sat 10am–6.15pm, Sun noon–6.15pm, winter until 5.15pm; nave free, charge for tombs; map E5
Stade de France, St-Denis; tel: 08 92 70 09 00; www.stadefrance.com; guided visits, times vary; charge: map E5

Picnic in the Domaine de St-Cloud with superb views of Paris across the Seine

Vistas and terraces, formal gardens and, above all, large expanses of grass and woodland make the **Domaine de St-Cloud** one of the loveliest places for a weekend stroll or a summer picnic, among the magnificent remains of a grand château park (minus the château, which burned down in 1870). Once the property of 'Monsieur' (Philippe d'Orléans, brother of Louis XIV), the park – landscaped by André Le Nôtre, the king's master gardener, also responsible for Versailles and the Tuileries – became a favourite setting for grand fêtes given by

19th-century royalty. There's a superb view of Paris across the Seine from the belvedere, and a network of fountains to rival Versailles are put into action accompanied by world music performances over a weekend in June. There are cafés, a small farm, a circus pitch and pedal cars, a grand fireworks spectacular in September, and one of France's best rock festivals, Rock en Seine, on the last weekend in August.

At the foot of the park is the Manufacture de Sèvres, the historic porcelain factory founded in the 18th century which still makes porcelain to historic designs from its archives (visits of the ateliers by rendezvous). Recently rebaptised Sèvres, Cité de la Céramique, the 25 listed buildings also include the **Musée National de la Céramique**, presenting a huge panorama of ceramics from around the world.

Domaine National de St-Cloud; St-Cloud; www.saint-cloud.monuments-nationaux. fr; daily summer 7.30am–9/10pm, winter 7.30am–8pm; charge for cars and motorbikes; map A1
Musée National de Sèvres; 2 place de la Manufacture, Sèvres; tel: 01 46 29 22 00; www.sevresciteceramique.fr; Wed–Mon 10am–5pm; charge; map A1

Climb a medieval skyscraper in Vincennes, then lie back to the sound of music in the park

Compared to the Louvre or Versailles, the one-time role of the **Château de Vincennes** as royal residence has been rather forgotten; but its restored *donjon* (keep) – at 50 metres (164ft) high, the tallest in France – imparts a vision of Charles V's ambition when he moved out of Ile de la Cité and turned a secondary residence of the Capetians into a powerful stronghold. After climbing the surrounding *châtelet*, where you can admire the view from the parapet walk, a bridge brings you to the keep, where Charles V's council room, with its vaulted ceiling and 3-metre (10ft-) thick walls, and the royal chamber up above, give a surprising sense of medieval palace life. Charles V also built the curtain wall (big enough to contain an entire town), and began the Ste Chapelle, a soaring Gothic edifice. The castle continued to be used by the monarchy, especially when things got too hot in Paris.

If you're here on a summer weekend, combine your visit with a concert in the **Parc Floral**, across the esplanade to the south. An excellent line up of jazz musicians in the **Paris Jazz Festival** (www.parisjazzfestival.fr) in June–July gives way to symphony orchestras and chamber music in **Classique au Vert** (www.classiqueauvert.fr) in August–September. There are some seats by the stage but most people laze on the lawns or lounge between flowerbeds across the lake. This modern botanical garden recreates different habitats – pinewood, oak forest, water lily pond, butterfly house, bonsai garden – as well as an amusing minigolf around the monuments of Paris.

Château de Vincennes; avenue de Paris, Vincennes; tel: 01 43 28 15 48; www.vincennes.monuments-nationaux.fr; daily mid-May–mid-Sept 10am–6pm, mid-Sept–mid-May 10am–5pm; charge; map G2
Parc Floral de Paris; Bois de Vincennes; daily summer 9.30am–8pm, winter 9.30am–5pm; free except charge Wed, Sat, Sun June–Sept; map G2

ESSENTIALS

A

ARRIVAL

By Air

Arriving from Paris Charles de Gaulle

Most international flights arrive at **Paris Charles de Gaulle airport** (www.aeroportsdeparis.fr), 27km (17 miles) north of the city.

The most reliable and inexpensive way into town is by **RER line B**, which takes around 45 minutes to Châtelet-Les Halles (€9.75). There are two stations: Aéroport Charles de Gaulle 1 serves Terminals 1 and 3; Aéroport Charles de Gaulle 2/TGV serves Terminal 2 and is also a mainline station for high-speed trains all over France. The free, driverless CDGVAL light railway connects the different terminals, RER stations and car parks.

There are also assorted bus services, including the **Roissybus** to Opéra (€11) and **Air France** coaches to Etoile/Porte Maillot and Montparnasse (€17).

Count on at least €50–70 for a taxi into town, plus supplements for each piece of luggage. **Paris Airport Shuttle** (www.paris-airport-shuttle.com), **Paris Shuttle** (www.parishuttle.com) and **Yellow Van Shuttle** (www.airport-connection.com) run minibus services between the airport and hotels (€75–90 per van). Allow plenty of time if you're planning to return by taxi or minibus.

Arriving from Paris Orly

A few flights arrive at the smaller **Orly airport** (www.aeroportsdeparis.fr), 14km (9 miles) south of the city centre. To reach Paris, take the Orlybus (€7.70) to Denfert-Rochereau station in Paris, every 15–20 minutes 6am–11.30pm. The costlier Orlyval automatic train (€9.30) is a shuttle to Antony (the nearest RER to Orly). It runs every 4–7 minutes, 6am–11pm, and takes 35 minutes. Allow around €40–55 for a taxi.

By Train

Eurostar (UK tel: 03432-186 186; www.eurostar.com; France tel: 0892 35 35 39) runs fast, frequent rail services from London (St Pancras) or Ebbsfleet station to Paris Gare du Nord. The service runs about 12 times a day and takes around 2 hours 15 mins.

By Car

There are frequent car ferries between Dover and Calais run by **DFDS** (UK tel: 0871 574 7235/France tel:+44 208 127 8303; www.dfdsseaways.co.uk) and **P&O Ferries** (UK tel: 0800 130 0030/France tel:03 66 74 03 25; www.poferries.com) or you can take **Le Shuttle** (UK tel: 08443-353 535/France tel: 08 10 63 03 04; www.eurotunnel.com) through the Channel Tunnel between Folkestone and Calais. It is 290km (180 miles) between Calais and Paris.

By Coach

National Express Eurolines (tel: 08717-818177; www.nationalexpress. com) runs services daily from London's Victoria Coach Station to Paris Gare Routière Galliéni, 28 avenue du Général-de-Gaulle, Bagnolet (tel: 08 92 89 90 91; www.eurolines.fr.), taking six to eight hours.

C

CLIMATE

The average maximum in July and August is 25°C (77°F), the average minimum 15°C (59°F), but 27°C (81°F) is not unusual. In January, expect a maximum of 6°C (43°F) and a minimum of 1°C (34°F). Snow is rare, but it can rain all year round, so bring an umbrella.

CRIME AND SAFETY

In the event of theft, a report must be made in person at the nearest police station (*commissariat*) as soon as possible. See www.prefecture-police-paris.interieur.gouv.fr for addresses of stations; for emergency help tel: 17.

If you lose your passport, report it to your consulate after notifying the police.

Security: It is advisable to take the same precautions in Paris as you would in any other major city, notably watching out for pickpockets on public transport and shielding your PIN at ATM machines. In the aftermath of the November 2015 terrorist attacks, expect security checks at museums, attractions and department stores.

D

DISABLED TRAVELLERS

The Disabled People Access section on the Paris tourist board website (www.parisinfo.com) has information on transport, equipment and services for the physically, mentally, sight or hearing disabled. It indicates where there is disabled access to sights, museums, hotels and restaurants, including the new national Tourisme et Handicaps labelling scheme (www. tourisme-handicaps.org).

UK Organisations: Disability Rights UK, Ground Floor, CAN Mezzanine, 49-51 East Road, London N1 6AH; tel: 0207 250 8181; www.disabilityrights uk.org.

US Organisations: Society for Accessible Travel and Hospitality (SATH), 347 Fifth Avenue, Suite 605, New York, NY 10016; tel: 212-447 7284; www.sath.org.

DRIVING

You probably won't want to drive in central Paris, which is well covered by public transport, but it can be useful for outer districts or suburbs. To drive in France, you must be at least 18. If you are bringing your own car, very few hotels have their own car parks, but they may offer special rates for a nearby car park.

To hire a car you will need to show your driving licence (held for at least a year) and passport. You will also need a major credit card, or a large deposit. The minimum age for renting cars is 21, although a young driver's supplement is usually payable for those under 25. Third-party insurance is compulsory, and full cover is recommended.

The major car hire companies all have branches at the main mainline stations and airports, including Avis (tel: 08 21 23 07 60; www.avis.fr/ UK tel: 0808 284 0014; www.avis.co.uk), Europcar (tel: 08 25 35 83 58; www. europcar.fr; UK tel: 0871 384 1087) and Hertz (tel: 01 41 91 95 25; www. hertz.fr; UK tel: 0207 026 0077).

E

ELECTRICITY

220-volt, 50-cycle AC is universal, with two-pin plugs. British visitors should buy an adaptor (adaptateur); American visitors will need a transformer (transformateur).

EMBASSIES AND CONSULATES

Australia: Embassy: 4 rue Jean-Rey, 15th; tel: 01 40 59 33 00; http://france. embassy.gov.au.
Canada: Embassy: 35 avenue Montaigne, 8th; tel: 01 44 43 29 00; www. canadainternational.gc.ca/france
Republic of Ireland: Embassy: 12 avenue Foch, 16th; tel: 01 44 17 67 00; www.embassyofireland.fr.
UK: Consulate: 16 rue d'Anjou, 8th; tel: 01 44 51 31 00; http://ukinfrance. fco.gov.uk/en.
US: Embassy: Consular Section, 4 avenue Gabriel, 1st; tel: 01 43 12 22 22; http://france.usembassy.gov.

EMERGENCY NUMBERS

Ambulance (SAMU): tel: 15
Fire brigade (pompiers): tel: 18
Police (police secours): tel: 17
All, from a mobile phone: tel: 112

G

GAY AND LESBIAN

Paris is generally gay-friendly, with the most visible gay community located in the Marais. The Centre Lesbien Gay Bi & Trans (63 rue Beaubourg, 3rd; tel: 01 43 57 21 47; www.centrelgbtparis.org) provides information and support and is an umbrella organisation for gay associations.

H

HEALTH

EU Nationals are eligible for medical treatment under the French health service. You will have to pay for the treatment, but are entitled to claim back up to 70 percent if you have a European Health Insurance Card (www.ehic.org.uk).

Non-EU visitors should take out health insurance.

The private American Hospital (Hôpital Américain de Paris, 63 boulevard Victor Hugo, Neuilly-sur-Seine; tel: 01 46 41 25 25; www.american-hospital.org) has a casualty service with bilingual staff.

Pharmacies

Most pharmacies open Monday to Saturday 9 or 10am to 7 or 8pm. On Sunday, they post the addresses of the nearest Sunday-opening pharmacies in their windows. A 24-hour pharmacy is Pharmacie Dhéry, 84 avenue des Champs-Elysées; tel: 01 45 62 02 41.

I

INTERNET

Most hotels have Wi-Fi access, which is usually free – check at the reception desk first. There is also free Wi-Fi in municipal parks, libraries, most museums and in train stations, as well as at some cafés.

24-hour internet café **Milk** (www.milklub.com) has two branches in Paris: 31 boulevard Sebastopol near Les Halles and 5 rue d'Odessa in Montparnasse.

L

LOST PROPERTY

To reclaim lost items in Paris, go in person (with ID) to the Bureau des Objets Trouvés, 36 rue des Morillons, 15th; tel: 08 21 00 25 25; Mon–Thur 8.30am–5pm, Fri 8.30am–4.30pm; metro: Convention.

M

MAPS

Most hotels can provide a basic foldout map, but if you really want to explore, it's worth investing in a small mapbook – such as **Paris pratique par arrondissement**, published by L'Indispensable, which covers the 20 *arrondissements*, or the larger *Maxi Paris*, which includes the inner suburbs. **Fleximap Paris**, published by Insight Guides, is a laminated fold-out map. Ask in metro stations for a map of the metro and bus routes.

MONEY

Currency. France uses the euro, divided into 100 centimes. Coins (*pièces*) come in one, two, five, 10, 20 and 50 *centimes*, and one and two euros. Banknotes (*billets*) come in five, 10, 20, 50, 100, 200 and 500 euros, but note that shops are often unwilling to accept the largest denomination notes.

Cash Machines. The easiest way to take out money is to use an ATM, with a debit or credit card such as Visa, MasterCard, Maestro or Cirrus, etc, and your PIN. Note that travellers' cheques are rarely used.

Credit Cards. Most shops, restaurants and hotels accept credit cards, especially Visa and MasterCard; there may be a minimum sum of 10 or 15 euros.

MUSEUMS AND MONUMENTS

The permanent collections are free at Paris's municipal museums, including the Petit Palais, the Musée Carnavalet, the Musée d'Art Moderne de la Ville de Paris, the Musée Cernuschi and the Maison de Victor Hugo, though you usually have to pay for temporary exhibitions.

Permanent collections at national museums, including the Louvre, the Musée d'Orsay, the Centre Pompidou, the Musée Rodin, and national monuments, such as the Arc de Triomphe and Sainte Chapelle, are free for all

EU residents/nationals aged under 26 (bring passport), for non-EU nationals under 18 if accompanied by an adult, and for everybody on the first Sunday of the month. Full admission prices usually vary between €10 and €15.

For independently owned museums, tariffs vary but are generally free for children under 12 or under 18.

If you are planning on some intensive museum-visiting, it may be worth investing in the Paris Museum Pass – which costs €48 for two days, €62 for four days and €74 for six days.

Most museums close on either Monday or Tuesday. Check before you go.

N

NEWSPAPERS AND MAGAZINES

The main daily newspapers are centre-left *Le Monde*, more conservative *Le Figaro* – which includes the *Figaroscope* listings supplement on Wednesdays – and left-slanted *Libération*. Less highbrow *Le Parisien* has a large section devoted to local news, the *Journal du Dimanche* is the main Sunday paper. Free newspapers distributed in or outside Métro stations include *Metro* and *Direct Matin*. Weekly news magazines include *Le Point*, *L'Express*, *Nouvel Observateur*, and more recent arrival *Marianne*. There are a vast number of consumer magazines but everyone likes to keep an eye on who's featured in *Paris Match*.

The British press is also widely available, as is *USA Today* and the Paris-based *International New York Times*.

P

POST AND STAMPS

Post Offices: Most branches open Mon–Fri 8am–7 or 8pm, Sat 8am–noon, sometimes with reduced hours in August. The central post office at 52 rue du Louvre, 1st, is open all night (Mon–Sat 7.30am–6am, Sun 10am–6am); www.laposte.fr. However, unless you are sending a parcel or registered post, it is usually easier to buy stamps (*timbres*) at a tobacconist (*tabac*).

PUBLIC HOLIDAYS (JOURS FÉRIÉS)

Banks, public buildings, and many museums and shops close on public holidays, during which transport runs on Sunday schedules.

1 Jan *Nouvel An* – New Year's Day
Mar/Apr *Lundi de Pâques* – Easter Monday
1 May *Fête du Travail* – Labour Day
8 May *Fête de la Victoire* – VE Day
Mid/late May *Ascension* – Ascension
Late May/early June *Lundi de Pentecôte* – Whit Monday
14 July *Le Quartorze Juillet* – Bastille Day
15 Aug *Fête de l'Assomption* – Assumption
1 Nov *Toussaint* – All Saints' Day
11 Nov *Le Onze Novembre* – Armistice Day, 1918
25 Dec *Noël* – Christmas

PUBLIC TRANSPORT

A generally efficient public transport system is run by the RATP (tel: 3424; www.ratp.fr), incorporating the metro, RER suburban express, buses and tramway.

Metro and RER

The metro has 14 lines. Services run from 5.30am to 12.30am, extended until around 1am on Friday and Saturday nights, with metros every two or three minutes at peak hours and more limited services on Sunday and bank holidays. The five **RER suburban express** lines go from central Paris far into the Ile-de-France suburbs, including the RER B to Aéroport Charles de Gaulle and the Stade de France. Within the city centre it can be useful for speedy journeys: for example Châtelet-Les Halles to Charles de Gaulle-Etoile is only two stops on the RER and seven stops by metro.

Buses and Trams

Some 50 bus routes criss-cross the city. It is a good way to see the city at ground level – and also a relatively efficient one, as sections of many routes now run in bus lanes. Some routes stop at around 9pm and not all routes run on Sunday.

In Montmartre, you can also take the Montmartrobus, capable of navigating the narrow streets of the *butte*, and the Funicular, which climbs up the side of square Willette to Sacré-Cœur. Both take standard RATP tickets or passes.

Night buses. 47 Noctilien night bus routes run – at rather long intervals – between central Paris and the suburbs from 12.30am to 5.30am, operating from five principal hubs at Châtelet, Gare St-Lazare, Gare Montparnasse, Gare de l'Est and Gare de Lyon.

The tram. Paris has nine modern tramlines (Line 4 is operated by the SNCF). Only line 3, which runs along the boulevards des Maréchaux on the Left Bank between Pont du Garigliano in the west and Porte de Vincennes in the east then up to Porte de la Chapelle in the north, is in Paris itself.

Tickets

The standard ticket (€1.80), designated t+, is valid on buses, métro and tramways, plus the RER within central Paris (zone 1). It allows changes on the metro network or between métro and RER or one change of bus or bus/tram within a period of 90 minutes (but not changes between métro and bus). It is usually simpler and more economical to buy a *carnet* of ten tickets (€14.10). Tickets should be validated when you get onto the bus or go through the metro barrier. Keep your ticket in case of spot inspections and to get out of RER stations. Separate tickets have to be bought for RER stations outside of the central zone and for airport buses.

If you are planning to use the bus or métro a lot, or to take the RER into the suburbs, another option is a one-day **Mobilis** ticket, priced according to number of zones. The **Paris Visite** pass, valid one, two, three, or five days, is aimed at tourists and covers either zones 1-3 or zones 1-6 (not including airports). It includes discounts on certain tourist attractions, although it often works out more expensive than a carnet or Mobilis pass.

Navigo. If you're staying for a longer time and are intending to use public transport regularly, you may want to buy a Navigo pass: a magnetic travelcard (photo required) available by the calendar month or weekly (valid Mon–Sun). The Passe Navigo is for residents of Paris and the Ile-de-France, the **Navigo Découverte** is available to anyone for an initial €5 plus the subscription.

Individual tickets, *carnets* and Navigo recharges can all be bought with cash or credit cards at ticket machines or ticket offices inside métro stations; *carnets* are available from some tobacconists too. Single-use tickets (€2) can also be bought from bus drivers but do not allow changes.

Vélib

Vélib (tel: 01 30 79 79 30; www.velib.paris.fr) is the enormously successful municipal bike hire scheme, with over 25,000 bikes and some 1,800 ranks in Paris and the inner suburbs. One- or seven-day subscriptions (€1.70/€8) can be taken out on the spot with a credit card. The first 30 minutes of each journey are free, it's €1 for the next 30 minutes and the rates rise sharply thereafter. There are a growing number of cycle lanes but note that while some are dedicated others are perilously shared with buses and taxis.

Taxis

Taxis can be hailed in the street or at taxi ranks, although are often in short supply as they tend to congregate at the airports and mainline stations. On old taxis, a white light on the roof indicates when it is free; a new more visible system is being introduced with a green light to indicate when the taxi is free and red when it is occupied. Rates differ according to the zones covered and time of day (there are higher rates between 5pm and 7am and on Sunday), and extra charges for luggage and for pick-up at a station or airport. Taxi drivers usually won't take more than three passengers. The fourth, if admitted, pays a supplement.

Central call centre 01 45 30 30 30; G7 taxis switchboard in English 01 41 27 66 99.

R

RESTAURANTS

Restaurants generally serve from around noon to around 2.30pm and from 7.30 or 8pm to around 10.30pm. If you want to eat outside these hours, your best bet is probably a café or brasserie, which often serve food all day and stay open until late. Cafés generally open at around 8am or 9am to serve breakfast. Many restaurants close on Monday and Sunday, and for all or part of August.

A service charge of 12-15 percent is always included in restaurant bills; any additional tip is purely optional, and bread and tap water are free. As well as à la carte dishes, many restaurants have good value menus at lunch time, and bistros often have a *menu-carte* system offering two or three courses for a fixed price.

S

SMOKING

Smoking is banned in all public buildings including stations, airports, museums, shops and offices, restaurants, bars and the public areas of hotels. Smoking is permitted in hotel bedrooms, unless designated non-smoking rooms, and on outdoor terraces at cafés and restaurants, or if they have a specially closed and ventilated *fumoir* (smoking room).

T

TELEPHONES

All telephone numbers in France have 10 digits. Paris and Ile-de-France numbers begin with 01. 06 numbers are for mobile phones. Numbers beginning 08 range from 0800 freephone numbers to premium rate calls. For the operator, call 12.

Directory enquiries are available from various providers, including 118000, 118008 and 118218 or use www.pagesjaune.fr.

Calling from Abroad. To dial Paris from abroad dial 00, followed by 33, the country code for France, followed by the Paris number, leaving off the 0 at the start. To call other countries from France, dial 00, then the country code: Australia 61, UK 44, US and Canada 1.

Public Telephone Boxes. Most phone boxes in Paris are operated with a card (*télécarte*), bought from tobacconists, newsstands and post offices; some also take credit/debit cards.

TIME ZONES

France is one hour ahead of Greenwich Mean Time (GMT) and six ahead of Eastern Standard Time.

TOURIST INFORMATION

Paris Convention and Visitors Bureau (25 rue des Pyramides, 1st; http://en.parisinfo.com; daily 9.30am–6.30pm). There are branches at Gare du Nord and Anvers (72 boulevard Rochechouart) open daily; 29 rue de Rivoli, Gare de l'Est and Gare de Lyon open Mon–Sat.

V

VISAS

All visitors to France require a valid passport. EU nationals do not need visas, nor do most visitors from the US, Australia, Canada and New Zealand if staying for less than 90 days. Nationals of other countries may need a visa; if in doubt, check with the French Consulate in your home country, or see www.diplomatie.gouv.fr.

INDEX

Experience Paris
Editor: Carine Tracanelli
Author: Natasha Edwards, Victoria Trott
Head of Production: Rebeka Davies
Picture Editor: Tom Smyth
Cartography: original cartography Apa
Cartography Department, updated by Carte
Photography: Alamy 31, 32, 37, 39, 40, 45,
52, 73, 88, 89, 92, 95, 105, 107, 120, 121,
138, 146, 150, 151, 153, 156, 157, 158;
Bouillon Chartier 62; Chantal Carousel 41;
Dreamstime 30; Four Seasons 79; Getty
Images 4/5, 6, 14T, 18B, 19, 33, 34/35, 36,
51, 60, 68/69, 70, 74, 76, 77, 78, 86, 91,
93, 100, 104, 109, 115, 117, 123, 139, 140,
144, 145, 160, 161, 162, 163; iStock 61,
124; Kevin Cummins/Apa Publications
13, 50, 57, 63, 94, 96, 101, 106, 116, 133,
154; Lasserre 71; Manuelle Gautrand
Architecture/Vincent Fillon 44; Ming Tang-
Evans/Apa Publications 8, 9, 10B, 10T, 11,
12, 14B, 15, 16B, 16T, 17, 18T, 21, 24, 29,
43, 46, 54, 55, 58, 64, 75, 80, 84, 85, 87, 90,
103, 110, 122, 125, 126, 128, 132, 134, 135,
137, 141, 142, 159; Musee Jacquemart 72;
Paul Cooper/REX/Shutterstock 53; Robert
Harding 119; Shutterstock 28, 56, 118,
143, 152
Cover: Getty Images

Distribution
UK, Ireland and Europe
Apa Publications (UK) Ltd
sales@insightguides.com
United States and Canada
Ingram Publisher Services
ips@ingramcontent.com
Australia and New Zealand
Woodslane
info@woodslane.com.au

Southeast Asia
Apa Publications (SN) Pte
singaporeoffice@insightguides.com
Hong Kong, Taiwan and China
Apa Publications (HK) Ltd
hongkongoffice@insightguides.com
Worldwide
Apa Publications (UK) Ltd
sales@insightguides.com

**Special Sales, Content Licensing
and CoPublishing**
Insight Guides can be purchased in bulk
quantities at discounted prices. We can
create special editions, personalised
jackets and corporate imprints tailored to
your needs.
sales@insightguides.com
www.insightguides.biz

First Edition 2016

Contact us
Every effort has been made to provide
accurate information in this publication,
but changes are inevitable. The publisher
cannot be responsible for any resulting
loss, inconvenience or injury. We would
appreciate it if readers would call our
attention to any errors or outdated
information. We also welcome your
suggestions; please contact us at:
hello@insightguides.com
www.insightguides.com

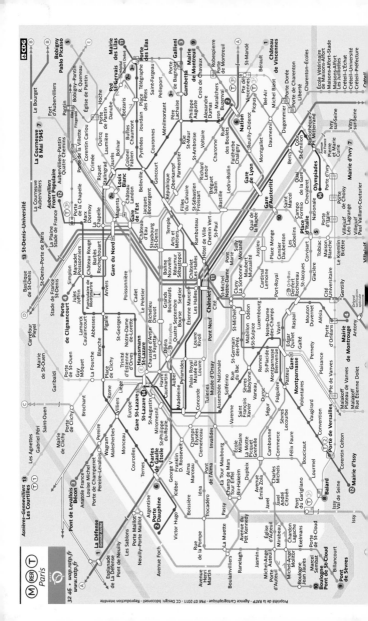

INSIGHT ◉ GUIDES
TRAVEL MADE EASY. ASK LOCAL EXPERTS.

UNIQUE HOLIDAYS, CHOSEN BY YOU
Dream it. Find it. Book it.

COLLECT YOUR VOUCHER
insightguides.com/books2016
code: BOOKS2016